EARLY CHILDHOOD EDUCATION SERIES

NANCY FILE & CHRISTOPHER P. BROWN, EDITORS

ADVISORY BOARD: Jie-Qi Chen, Cristina Gillanders, Jacqueline Jones,
Kristen M. Kemple, Candace R. Kuby, John Nimmo,
Amy Noelle Parks, Michelle Salazar Pérez, Andrew J. Stremmel, Valora Washington

---

Relationship-Based Care for Infants and Toddlers:
Fostering Early Learning and Development Through
Responsive Practice
SUSAN L. RECCHIA, MINSUN SHIN, & ELENI LOIZOU

Infants and Toddlers at Work: Using Reggio-
Inspired Materials to Support Brain Development,
Second Edition
ANN LEWIN-BENHAM

Leading Anti-Bias Early Childhood Programs:
A Guide to Change, for Change, 2nd Ed.
LOUISE DERMAN-SPARKS, DEBBIE LEEKEENAN,
& JOHN NIMMO

We Are the Change We Seek: Advancing Racial
Justice in Early Care and Education
IHEOMA U. IRUKA, TONIA R. DURDEN, KERRY-ANN
ESCAYG, & STEPHANIE M. CURENTON

Young Investigators:
The Project Approach in the Early Years, 4th Ed.
JUDY HARRIS HELM, LILIAN G. KATZ,
& REBECCA WILSON

Emotionally Responsive Teaching: Expanding
Trauma-Informed Practice With Young Children
TRAVIS WRIGHT

Rooted in Belonging:
Critical Place-Based Learning in Early Childhood
and Elementary Teacher Education
MELISSA SHERFINSKI WITH SHARON HAYES

Transforming Early Years Policy in the U.S.:
A Call to Action
MARK K. NAGASAWA, LACEY PETERS,
MARIANNE N. BLOCH, & BETH BLUE SWADENER, EDS.

Music Therapy With Preschool Children on the
Autism Spectrum: Moments of Meeting
GEOFF BARNES

On Being and Well-Being in Infant/Toddler Care
and Education: Life Stories From Baby Rooms
MARY BENSON MCMULLEN

Principals as Early Learning Leaders: Effectively
Supporting Our Youngest Learners
JULIE NICHOLSON, HELEN MANIATES, SERENE YEE,
THOMAS WILLIAMS JR., VERONICA UFOEGBUNE,
& RAUL ERAZO-CHAVEZ

Resisting the Kinder-Race:
Restoring Joy to Early Learning
CHRISTOPHER P. BROWN

Reshaping Universal Preschool:
Critical Perspectives on Power and Policy
LUCINDA GRACE HEIMER & ANN ELIZABETH
RAMMINGER, WITH KATHERINE K. DELANEY, SARAH
GALANTER-GUZIEWSKI, LACEY PETERS,
& KRISTIN WHYTE

Pre-K Stories: Playing with Authorship and
Integrating Curriculum in Early Childhood
DANA FRANTZ BENTLEY & MARIANA SOUTO-
MANNING

Ready or Not: Early Care and Education's
Leadership Choices—12 Years Later, 2nd Ed.
STACIE G. GOFFIN & VALORA WASHINGTON

Teaching STEM in the Preschool Classroom:
Exploring Big Ideas with 3- to 5-Year-Olds
ALISSA A. LANGE, KIMBERLY BRENNEMAN,
& HAGIT MANO

High-Quality Early Learning for a Changing World:
What Educators Need to Know and Do
BEVERLY FALK

Guiding Principles for the New Early Childhood
Professional: Building on Strength and Competence
VALORA WASHINGTON & BRENDA GADSON

Leading for Change in Early Care and Education:
Cultivating Leadership from Within
ANNE L. DOUGLASS

When Pre-K Comes to School: Policy, Partnerships,
and the Early Childhood Education Workforce
BETHANY WILINSKI

Continuity in Children's Worlds: Choices and
Consequences for Early Childhood Settings
MELISSA M. JOZWIAK, BETSY J. CAHILL,
& RACHEL THEILHEIMER

The Early Intervention Guidebook for Families and
Professionals: Partnering for Success, 2nd Ed.
BONNIE KEILTY

STEM Learning with Young Children:
Inquiry Teaching with Ramps and Pathways
SHELLY COUNSELL ET AL.

For a complete list of series titles, visit https://www.tcpress.

Early Childhood Education Series, *continued*

Courageous Leadership in Early Childhood
Education: Taking a Stand for Social Justice
  SUSI LONG ET AL., EDS.

Teaching Kindergarten
  JULIE DIAMOND ET AL., EDS.

The New Early Childhood Professional
  VALORA WASHINGTON ET AL.

Teaching and Learning in a Diverse World, 4th Ed.
  PATRICIA G. RAMSEY

In the Spirit of the Studio, 2nd Ed.
  LELLA GANDINI ET AL., EDS.

Exploring Mathematics Through Play in the Early
Childhood Classroom
  AMY NOELLE PARKS

Becoming Young Thinkers
  JUDY HARRIS HELM

The Early Years Matter
  MARILOU HYSON & HEATHER BIGGAR TOMLINSON

Thinking Critically About Environments for Young
Children
  LISA P. KUH, ED.

Standing Up for Something Every Day
  BEATRICE S. FENNIMORE

FirstSchool
  SHARON RITCHIE & LAURA GUTMANN, EDS.

Early Childhood Education for a New Era
  STACIE G. GOFFIN

Everyday Artists
  DANA FRANTZ BENTLEY

Multicultural Teaching in the Early Childhood
Classroom
  MARIANA SOUTO-MANNING

Inclusion in the Early Childhood Classroom
  SUSAN L. RECCHIA & YOON-JOO LEE

Moral Classrooms, Moral Children, 2nd Ed.
  RHETA DEVRIES & BETTY ZAN

Defending Childhood
  BEVERLY FALK, ED.

Starting with Their Strengths
  DEBORAH C. LICKEY & DENISE J. POWERS

The Play's the Thing
  ELIZABETH JONES & GRETCHEN REYNOLDS

Twelve Best Practices for Early Childhood
Education
  ANN LEWIN-BENHAM

Big Science for Growing Minds
  JACQUELINE GRENNON BROOKS

What If All the Kids Are White? 2nd Ed.
  LOUISE DERMAN-SPARKS & PATRICIA G. RAMSEY

Seen and Heard
  ELLEN LYNN HALL & JENNIFER KOFKIN RUDKIN

Connecting Emergent Curriculum and Standards in
the Early Childhood Classroom
  SYDNEY L. SCHWARTZ & SHERRY M. COPELAND

Infants and Toddlers at Work
  ANN LEWIN-BENHAM

The View from the Little Chair in the Corner
  CINDY RZASA BESS

Culture and Child Development in Early Childhood
Programs
  CAROLLEE HOWES

Educating and Caring for Very Young Children,
2nd Ed.
  DORIS BERGEN ET AL.

Beginning School
  RICHARD M. CLIFFORD & GISELE M. CRAWFORD, EDS.

Emergent Curriculum in the Primary Classroom
  CAROL ANNE WIEN, ED.

Enthusiastic and Engaged Learners
  MARILOU HYSON

Powerful Children
  ANN LEWIN-BENHAM

The Early Care and Education Teaching Workforce
at the Fulcrum
  SHARON LYNN KAGAN ET AL.

Supervision in Early Childhood Education, 3rd Ed.
  JOSEPH J. CARUSO WITH M. TEMPLE FAWCETT

Guiding Children's Behavior
  EILEEN S. FLICKER & JANET ANDRON HOFFMAN

The War Play Dilemma, 2nd Ed.
  DIANE E. LEVIN & NANCY CARLSSON-PAIGE

Possible Schools
  ANN LEWIN-BENHAM

Everyday Goodbyes
  NANCY BALABAN

Playing to Get Smart
  ELIZABETH JONES & RENATTA M. COOPER

The Emotional Development of Young Children,
2nd Ed.
  MARILOU HYSON

Young Children Continue to Reinvent Arithmetic—
2nd Grade, 2nd Ed.
  CONSTANCE KAMII

Bringing Learning to Life
  LOUISE BOYD CADWELL

A Matter of Trust
  CAROLLEE HOWES & SHARON RITCHIE

Bambini
  LELLA GANDINI & CAROLYN POPE EDWARDS, EDS.

Young Children Reinvent Arithmetic, 2nd Ed.
  CONSTANCE KAMII

Bringing Reggio Emilia Home
  LOUISE BOYD CADWELL

Relationship-Based Care for Infants and Toddlers

Fostering Early Learning and Development Through Responsive Practice

Susan L. Recchia, Minsun Shin,
and Eleni Loizou

Foreword by Mary Benson McMullen

Teachers College Press
TEACHERS COLLEGE | COLUMBIA UNIVERSITY
NEW YORK AND LONDON

*This book is dedicated to the infants, toddlers, families,
and caring teachers who have taught us so much
about the power of authentic relationships and
the meaning of responsive practice.*

Published by Teachers College Press,® 1234 Amsterdam Avenue, New York, NY 10027

Copyright © 2023 by Teachers College, Columbia University

Front cover design by Holly Grundon / BHG Graphics. Photos (clockwise from top): Igor Alecsander / iStock by Getty Images; santypan / Shutterstock; FatCamera / iStock by Getty Images; FatCamera / iStock by Getty Images

All rights reserved. No part of this publication may be reproduced or transmitted in any form or by any means, electronic or mechanical, including photocopy, or any information storage and retrieval system, without permission from the publisher. For reprint permission and other subsidiary rights requests, please contact Teachers College Press, Rights Dept.: tcpressrights@tc.columbia.edu

Library of Congress Cataloging-in-Publication Data

Names: Recchia, Susan, author. | Shin, Minsun, author. | Loizou, Eleni, author.
Title: Relationship-based care for infants and toddlers : fostering early learning
  and development through responsive practice / Susan L. Recchia, Minsun Shin,
  and Eleni Loizou ; foreword by Mary Benson McMullen.
Description: New York : Teachers College Press, [2023] | Series: Early childhood
  education series | Includes bibliographical references and index. | Summary:
  "Through vignettes from the authors' research and practice, the social and
  emotional worlds of babies and toddlers and their caregivers come to life.
  Readers will explore the elements needed for professional preparation, including
  overarching principles of relationship-based practice"—Provided by publisher.
Identifiers: LCCN 2023011719 (print) | LCCN 2023011720 (ebook) |
  ISBN 9780807768907 (paper : acid-free paper) | ISBN 9780807768914
  (hardcover : acid-free paper) | ISBN 9780807782002 (ebook)
Subjects: LCSH: Early childhood education. | Child development. | Child care.
Classification: LCC LB1139.23 .R398 2023 (print) | LCC LB1139.23 (ebook) |
  DDC 372.21—dc23/eng/20230613
LC record available at https://lccn.loc.gov/2023011719
LC ebook record available at https://lccn.loc.gov/2023011720

ISBN 978-0-8077-6890-7 (paper)
ISBN 978-0-8077-6891-4 (hardcover)
ISBN 978-0-8077-8200-2 (ebook)

Printed on acid-free paper
Manufactured in the United States of America

Contents

Foreword *Mary Benson McMullen*   ix

1. **The Social and Emotional World of Infant–Toddler Childcare**   1

   Introduction   1

   The Power of Relationships as a Context for Social and
   Emotional Learning   5

   Overarching Principles That Guide Relationship-Based Practice   6

   Overview With Brief Chapter Descriptions   7

   Chapter Summary   9

PART I: DISTINCTIVE INFANT–TODDLER SOCIAL ENCOUNTERS IN CHILDCARE

2. **Infant–Toddler Play as an Essential Component of Early Learning
   and Development**   13

   Infants' and Toddlers' Ways of Learning   13

   Infants' and Toddlers' Play Experiences   15

   Infant–Toddler Play Practices and the Caregiver Role   22

   Discussion Questions   29

3. **Friendships Among Infant–Toddler Peers**   30

   Infant–Toddler Friendships   31

   Friendship Experiences and Sociocultural Context   36

   Infant–Toddler Caregiving to Support Friendships and
   Social Experiences   39

   Discussion Questions   42

vi   Contents

4. Creative Social Exchanges: Infant–Toddler Humor   **43**

Humor Definition and Theories   43

Peer Social Encounters as a Catalyst for Humor Development   50

Classroom Learning Environments and Caregiver Roles
Support Humor   52

Discussion Questions   57

**PART II: CREATING INTERPERSONAL ENVIRONMENTS
THAT SUPPORT RESPONSIVE CARE**

**5. The Complex Role of Infant–Toddler Professionals:
Care, Love, Diversity, and Identities**   **61**

Bringing Care, Education, and Love Together   62

Contemplating Emotional Labor   66

Appreciating Diverse Lived Experiences   69

Discussion Questions   73

**6. Becoming an Infant–Toddler Teacher: Ways of Thinking and
Ways of Being**   **74**

Relationship-Based Care and the Primary Care System   75

Being With and Learning From Infants and Toddlers   77

Becoming an Infant–Toddler Practitioner Within a
Supportive Learning Community   82

Discussion Questions   90

**7. Constellations of Care: Building Caring Infant–Toddler
Communities**   **91**

Constellations of Caring/Ethic of Care   92

Valuing Inclusive Practice/Honoring Differences   96

Respecting and Supporting New and Continuing Transitions   98

Capitalizing on Opportunities to Build Community Among Staff,
Children, and Families   100

Making Administrative and Policy Decisions That Reflect
Relationship-Based Practice   102

Contents   vii

Discussion Questions   104

8. Enduring Reflections for the Field of Infant–Toddler Care and Education   105

Infants and Toddlers as Being and Becoming   105

Infants' and Toddlers' Rights to Responsive and Loving Care   107

Infant–Toddler Care as a "Home" for Fostering Community and Subjective Well-Being   109

Concluding Thoughts   110

References   **111**

Index   **127**

About the Authors   **133**

Foreword

Infants and toddlers are competent and innately motivated to learn.

As I read this book, I marveled at how very far we have come in understanding and appreciating babyhood! We have journeyed well beyond the ideas of early philosophers such as John Locke (1632–1704) and his image of infants as "empty vessels" and their minds as "blank slates," and Jean-Jacques Rousseau's (1712–1788) view of them as "helpless" and "weak." We have grown so much since progressive thinkers such as Maria Montessori (1870–1952) asserted that children are only capable of communication after they have acquired language and medical scientists of the late 20th century claimed they did not feel pain until their first birthday. These archaic views of infancy and many others have been replaced by knowledge of babies, as our authors say, as "competent and innately motivated to learn," deserving of human rights and of our full respect. Not only do newborns have their own unique temperaments, but they are fully sensing beings who begin learning about the world even before birth and are fully able to communicate, if only we pay attention. They are endowed from the very beginning with a multitude of gifts, traits, and ways of responding that draw us in. They are born ready to do what is essential for survival and to being human: Relate to others.

Drs. Susan L. Recchia, Minsun Shin, and Eleni Loizou masterfully interweave relevant theory and research with insightful personal stories and vignettes in this brilliant book about relationship-based practices with infants and toddlers, as well as their families and teachers. The work is compelling and highly engaging as well as informative. Early childhood scholars, teacher educators, practitioners, and students will find this work useful and appreciate it for its thorough coverage and synthesis of the research—a culmination of decades of evidence about the power of forming relationships and sensitive responsiveness and the impact of this on the growth, development, learning, and well-being of children from birth to age 3. Importantly, the authors also add refreshingly new information to the literature that readers will find interesting. I was particularly fascinated by their descriptions of infant–toddler friendships and captivated by their accounts of infant humor, much of the research for which was compiled over recent years by the authors themselves. These topics and more, along with the authors' highly readable writing style, makes this book an ideal resource to share with families, community members, and policymakers about why we must prioritize relationship-based care.

There is so much in this book that is noteworthy, including the deep respect demonstrated for those who spend their lives devoted to the care and education of infants and toddlers and their families. Although we still have a distance to travel in our society toward fully valuing these professionals, the authors inspire hope. They honor the dignity of this work that leads babies to come to understand themselves and others. They reframe and further debunk discourses that undervalue this work of caring for, educating, and, yes, even loving babies as less than a professional pursuit. To Susan, Minsun, and Eleni I say, "Three cheers!" for recognizing and elevating infant toddler professionals for the "physical, mental, and highly emotional work" (p. 69) that they do.

In addition, rather than shying away from some of the debates in our field, the authors take them on, justifying their perspectives using their decades of experience as practitioners, researchers, and teacher educators. One such important discussion is the debate of whether infant–toddler work is "care" or "education," and they conclude, rather hopefully, "the field of early childhood education and care has come to acknowledge that there should be no division between care and education" (p. 61). And although I think this statement may be true among those of us considered to be baby scholars and practitioners, most of the population sees caregivers as "less than" based on their chosen profession. But the authors make me hopeful this can and will change!

In addition, Susan, Minsun, and Eleni examine the contested view of the role of "love" in the field. They consider both sides of the debate in the field about whether infant–toddler professionals can, do, or should "love" babies and what it looks like if they do. They point out that this important way of relating to and engaging with babies is all too often "invisible and silenced" (p. 61).

I find their views on and assertions of the importance of "care," "love," and "being and well-being" to be refreshing and thought-provoking. As I write, I despair for our society, as I see it so fraught with divisiveness and incivility, and so many of its people full of fear, anger, and even hate for others. Susan, Minsun, and Eleni remind us of the importance of prioritizing human relationships from the very beginning, that learning to be compassionate, empathetic, and kind starts within the relationships babies have from their earliest days. We who engage in infant–toddler work within our own "constellations of care" at all levels need to read and take to heart the messages in this book.

—Mary Benson McMullen

CHAPTER 1

The Social and Emotional World of Infant–Toddler Childcare

In this chapter we introduce the core content of this book: the social and emotional world of infant–toddler childcare. We set the stage for the chapters that follow by highlighting foundational knowledge from research and practice that illuminates how early learning unfolds for children through social and emotional experience, how infant–toddler professionals come to support and engage in infants' and toddlers' social worlds, and how early care and education settings create a nurturing space for children, families, and practitioners through enactments of relationship-based care. We introduce ourselves as authors, sharing our experiences and perspectives grounded in our years of practice as infant–toddler teachers and teacher educators. Finally, we provide a brief description of the chapters within each section of the book, as a roadmap for our readers.

INTRODUCTION

In this book, we bring to life the social worlds of diverse babies and toddlers, their peers, and their caregivers as they emerge within relationship-based infant–toddler childcare. We focus on children from birth to 3 years of age, alternating terms such as "baby," "infant," or "infant–toddler" to refer to children in the first 3 years of life. Chapters are designed to inform and enhance conceptualizations of infants and toddlers as unique social beings and partners, teachers and learners, and members of a childcare community. We reflect children's, families', and teachers' experiences in early care and education settings that are inclusive and culturally and linguistically diverse, highlighting contexts within which a variety of relationship-based social connections are nurtured and supported.

Unlike other texts that may provide a traditional linear approach to infant developmental milestones or a list of decontextualized strategies for infant–toddler teachers to apply, this text offers a nonprescriptive way of seeing how social and emotional experiences unfold in the everyday moments of infant–toddler childcare (Shin, 2010). Throughout the text, we share images

1

of infants and toddlers as active, agentic, and intentional social partners from the start of life, highlighting their unique capacities for social engagement with both adults and peers (Loizou, 2005a). Interwoven within each chapter's narrative are insights culled from extensive observations, teacher interviews, and video analyses during our years of research and practice.

We begin by introducing the overarching relationship-based framework within which the following chapters unfold. We focus in the first part of the text on infants' and toddlers' social lives within childcare, with a particular emphasis on play, friendships, and humor (Loizou, 2005a; Loizou & Recchia, 2019; Shin, 2010) as essential elements of infant–toddler learning. Building on these aspects of babies' ways of being in group care, we turn in the second part of the text to the role that professionals play in supporting infants' and toddlers' social development and learning. We address the complex roles of infant–toddler professionals (Shin, 2021b), the critical elements needed for in-depth and specialized professional preparation, and the overarching principles of relationship-based practice as applied to work with diverse families, policies, and practices in building caring childcare communities.

In this introductory chapter we briefly describe our perspectives as both teacher educators and qualitative researchers deeply engaged in the study of infant childcare and the preparation of infant professionals. We introduce ourselves and our philosophical beliefs grounded in our years of practice. In the chapters that follow, we incorporate the voices of preservice and in-service teachers, reflecting their experiences as they learned to teach and care for infants and toddlers in childcare. Observational anecdotes of children in action bring their ways of being to life, and family perspectives are shared.

Who We Are and Why This Book?

Susan. I always tell my students that my interest in infants emerged when my mother had twins when I was 9 years old. I remember watching intently as they slept side by side in one crib as newborns; I could hardly wait for them to wake up! I was so fascinated by their ways of responding and how different they were. My brother was bigger and stronger than my sister and had a very different personality from the start. As they grew, I spent many hours playing with and caring for them. Through our growing relationships, I discovered the unique ways they had of communicating their needs and interests and expressing their emotions, and how important it was to adapt my ways of responding to them. They taught me so much about early learning and development and inspired a lifelong career.

As an undergraduate, I was fortunate to find work as an assistant teacher at our university childcare center. There I learned from two amazing teachers how to build on my intuitive knowledge to engage in relationship-based infant–toddler care and education for a group of children in childcare. After graduation, I worked as an infant teacher and then as director at a small infant–toddler center established by a group of parents as a cooperative. Families were involved in all aspects of running the center and spent time each week volunteering alongside the staff.

Several years later, I transitioned to early childhood special education and worked as an infant specialist, focusing on families and children with disabilities. I learned how to listen to families on a deeper level and partner with them in teaching and caring for their children. I learned how to look beyond an initial formal assessment to really see the whole child, and to pay careful attention to their ways of being in the world and what they are capable of as opposed to what they have not yet achieved.

Later, when I became an early childhood teacher educator, I drew on all these experiences as I crafted my courses and supervised my students in the field. I was very fortunate to find a home as faculty director of the Rita Gold Early Childhood Center at Teachers College, Columbia University, soon after my arrival. There I worked directly with teachers and families throughout the center and taught and supervised students in the infant–toddler practicum course. My research over many years included ongoing study of how preservice teachers engage in working with infants and toddlers, learning from their reflections and insights. This work has continued to fuel my passionate interest in discovering better ways to provide high-quality responsive care for infants, toddlers, and families and in preparing infant–toddler teachers to understand and engage in authentic relationship-based practice.

Minsun. When I was in the master's program at Teachers College, Columbia University, I was pretty sure I wanted to become a child psychologist. With a motive to learn more about young children's development, I visited the Center for Infants and Parents on campus, which later grew to become the Rita Gold Early Childhood Center. I was advised to take an infant practicum course to learn more about babies. That was how everything started.

At first, I was extremely nervous as it was my first experience working with babies and my first teaching experience in the United States. My meeting with Susan (a director of the Center and a practicum professor) made me realize that infants would get to know my heart, not just what I say or "teach." I love how educators look at each child's strengths and work from there. I learned that teaching is more about taking care of the human being. That conversation and my practicum experiences changed and transformed my entire perspective on teaching and my course of life.

During my time at the Center and doctoral study in early childhood education, I was fortunate to work closely with Susan and Eleni. I worked at the Center for several years. I wore different hats, such as practicum student-teacher, supervising caregiver, graduate fellow, research member, and later a parent. I was fascinated by infants' capabilities to connect with people around them. Thus, I chose infant friendship as a topic for my doctoral dissertation. Then, other doctoral study students kept asking with such puzzling eyes, *"What? How can infants have friendships? How will you measure that?"* I was shocked. People do not know the amazing world of infants, I thought. The concepts from studies of older children were often extrapolated and applied to infants. I felt a compelling need to challenge the view of infants as incapable, powerless, and entirely dependent. Mentored by Susan with such caring guidance and immense love, I began to explore infants' capabilities and how infant teachers facilitate the infants' optimal level of development and learning.

I am an associate professor at Montclair State University in New Jersey. My experiences with babies have tremendously influenced my current teaching and scholarship activities. I truly believe that education takes place in and through human relationships. Thus, it is crucial to get to know my students, encourage interaction and human conversation, provide a challenging yet supportive learning environment, and support them to become lifelong learners as I learn alongside them. I advocate for a relationship-based approach in working with students, whether they are infants or college students.

Eleni. I am a professor of early childhood education at the University of Cyprus. As an early childhood education teacher, my theoretical and practical experiences have been in early years focusing on children ages 3–6 years old. During my undergraduate and master's level studies, I developed a strong pedagogic identity of an early childhood education teacher who focuses on play and enhances learning through different content areas.

During my doctoral studies, I was truly lucky to meet Susan and Minsun, who were my mentors and guided me in the world of infants and toddlers. My first baby experiences, working and researching infants and toddlers at the Rita Gold Center of Teachers' College, facilitated me in developing an infancy pedagogy; it is one based on relationships. I was provided with time and space to transition from early years to infancy, an experience that took a lot of reflection and reconceptualization of pedagogy and praxis. I was intrigued by the babies' interactions and behaviors; every lunch time, two boys found ways to make each other laugh, such as by moving their heads, dropping their water cup, or making funny faces. I decided to focus my doctoral thesis on infant humor. So, guided by Susan, I explored infant–toddler humor, an experience that further expanded my understanding of babies and their amazing abilities and potential.

Also, as a mother of three, I have come to deeply live, observe, and explore their learning and development, as the most thought-provoking, fascinating research and pedagogic experience. Finally, as a professor of early childhood education, I teach an infancy course where I guide students during their practicum experiences in childcare settings to focus on the pedagogy of infants and make the same transition I experienced during my doctoral studies. Additionally, I am involved in various research projects at my Early Childhood Research Lab with parents and babies, and I organize professional development programs with in-service infant–toddler teachers in Cyprus supporting responsive educare.

THE POWER OF RELATIONSHIPS AS A CONTEXT FOR SOCIAL AND EMOTIONAL LEARNING

Interdisciplinary research has redefined our understanding of even the youngest children's capacity for social and emotional learning. Once considered passive recipients of the environment, we now see infants and toddlers as active social beings predisposed to learning from others and from the experiences they encounter in their everyday lives (Lally, 2013; Shonkoff & Phillips, 2000). Infants' and toddlers' social and emotional competencies have been underestimated and have not been studied adequately within the context of group care settings.

The unique characteristics of infants and toddlers, including their preverbal communication systems, an increased need for physical care and emotional nurturing, and the use of bodily and sensory exploration as a primary means of discovery (Loizou, 2007), were once seen as limitations to more sophisticated learning rather than the powerful learning tools that they are (Shin, 2021a). Innovative medical technologies have allowed us access to in-depth study of the human brain, illuminating infants' social understanding, and giving new meaning to their engagement with both adults and peers from the beginning of life (Fogel, 2009).

Authentic and Meaningful Relationships as an Essential Framework for Early Learning

Infants' complex ways of making sense of their social worlds has brought to light a critical need to conceptualize their care environments within a relationship context, building on their natural abilities for interpersonal engagement. Early childhood scholars argue for implementing a relationship-based approach to teaching and caring for infants and toddlers (Degotardi & Pearson, 2014; Lally, 2013), as sensitive and responsive relationships in childcare have been consistently correlated with advanced levels of cognitive, language, and social skills in young children (National Institute of Child Health and Human Development Early Child Care Research Network, 2001; Institute of Medicine and National Research Council, 2015). However, little is known about the process through which relationship-based care evolves in practice (Lee, 2006; Recchia & Shin, 2010; Shin, 2015), how it adapts to accommodate cultural and learning differences, or how relationships in infant–toddler childcare extend beyond the adult–child dyad. Established guidelines for infant–toddler care and education frequently prioritize structural and health and safety needs without fully addressing and supporting the social and emotional foundations of early learning (Lally, 2013).

Attachments With Adults and Peers

Research on attachment relationships and their significance in early development has focused primarily on parents and their infants and toddlers, but much of this work began before infant–toddler childcare was as widespread as it is today. Studies on relationships between young children and their childcare teachers have shown that infants and toddlers are quite capable of forming attachments to multiple caregivers, including those outside of their immediate families. These relationships have a meaningful impact on their social, emotional, and learning experiences in childcare (Howes & Hamilton, 1992, 1993; Howes & Ritchie, 2002). Close relationships with infant–toddler caregivers who provide responsive, respectful, reliable, and trusted care, consistently and over time, have been shown to provide optimal pathways to growth and development (Gloeckler & La Paro, 2016).

Infants and toddlers develop their own unique ways of communicating, just as caregivers bring their own personal styles to the relationship. Together they learn to engage in a reciprocal dialogue with each other (Degotardi & Pearson, 2014), becoming social and emotional partners. This process works best when caregivers have a true desire to know the infants and toddlers in their care, and when they "approach care with a sense of wonder rather than a sense of knowing" (Petrie & Owen, 2005, p. 84). Over time, infant–toddler relationships with their caregivers will evolve as children gain new skills, requiring their caregivers to respond in more sophisticated ways (Goouch & Powell, 2013; Jung & Recchia, 2013; Recchia & Shin, 2012).

Infants and toddlers in childcare have many opportunities to develop relationships not only with a group of adults outside of their families but also with their peers. When even the youngest children come together in groups where they feel safe and well cared for, they begin to see themselves as part of a larger community (Recchia & Fincham, 2019). As you read further in this book, you will find many examples of the ways that infant–toddler peers make meaningful connections with each other in childcare settings. They look to each other for joint play experiences, appreciate and learn from each other's perspectives, and may find security and comfort in being with peers at stressful times (Recchia & Dvorakova, 2012).

OVERARCHING PRINCIPLES THAT GUIDE
RELATIONSHIP-BASED PRACTICE

Infant–toddler childcare provides unique opportunities for social and emotional learning, not only for children but for their families and caregivers as well. When infant–toddler childcare centers immerse themselves in an inclusive and caring framework that guides all aspects of practice, they create a dynamic presence for everyone involved. Questions or issues that arise are responded to through this lens, respecting individual differences while working to solve problems together.

Recchia and Fincham (2019) have described a set of overarching principles that has guided their work with infants and toddlers at the Rita Gold Early Childhood Center over many years. These principles include the following:

1. Human relationships are prioritized throughout the caregiving system.
2. Families are the primary caregivers and educators of their children.
3. Infants and toddlers are competent and innately motivated to learn.
4. An integrated, responsive curriculum strengthens infants' and toddlers' sense of self and their potential for learning and development.
5. Caregivers respect and appreciate infants' and toddlers' ways of being and sense of time.
6. Childcare centers foster community, belonging, and subjective well-being.

When doubts arise about our practices or we are faced with professional dilemmas, we return to these principles to guide our decisions. As you read further, you will find that these principles are reflected in our chapters through anecdotes and vignettes that bring day-to-day experiences of infant–toddler childcare to life.

OVERVIEW WITH BRIEF CHAPTER DESCRIPTIONS

Each chapter in Part I is guided by a clear set of constructs focusing on relationships as an essential context for infant and toddler development and care, the integral nature of play as a facilitator of infant–toddler teaching and learning, infants' individual contributions to their own learning and development, and teachers' ways of supporting and nurturing social and emotional experiences for infants and toddlers in childcare. Rather than bombarding our readers with theories of child development, our aim is to bring theoretical ideas to life through stories and anecdotes from practice, providing images of relationship-based care that illuminate infants', toddlers', and teachers' ways of being in actual childcare settings. To ensure anonymity, we have changed the names of individuals and places throughout the book.

In Chapter 2, "Infant–Toddler Play as an Essential Component of Early Learning and Development," we focus on play as the primary context for early learning for infants and toddlers. We use anecdotes to illustrate how careful observation of infants and toddlers gives rise to more meaningful, responsive, and playful relationship-based pedagogy. Through play, infants find agency as they explore the world alongside their caregivers and peers. We uncover the ways that caregivers support learning through play as partners, scaffolders, responders, observers, and recorders of infant–toddler play in their everyday childcare practice.

Chapter 3, "Friendships Among Infant–Toddler Peers," elucidates the ways that very young children establish friendships with their peers and how those friendships come to life in childcare. Through anecdotes describing the unique ways that friendships emerge and evolve, we reveal how these special reciprocal peer relationships contribute to infant–toddler social and emotional learning. We discuss the role that caregivers play as potential supporters and scaffolders of infant–toddler friendships, and the ways they can contribute to this aspect of relationship-based pedagogy in childcare.

Chapter 4, "Creative Social Exchanges: Infant–Toddler Humor," focuses on the emergence of humor as an integral part of creative social exchanges and playful, responsive pedagogy for infants, toddlers, and caregivers. We describe infants' and toddlers' ways of appreciating and producing humor through their unique words and actions, illustrating how humor encompasses critical aspects of social and cognitive development and learning. The crucial role of caregivers and the classroom environment in supporting humor development is also explored.

The chapters in Part II build on the underlying principles of relationship-based care as foundational in considering issues of professional preparation, policy, and practice in creating caring childcare communities. In this section we begin to explore the components that help build childcare environments that can enact the kinds of teaching and caring practices with infants, toddlers, and families described in Part I. We share what we've learned about the complexity of working with this age group, the challenges of group care for diverse infants and toddlers and their families, the process of becoming an infant–toddler caregiver, and the dilemmas around professional identities. Stories from the field grounded in our research and practice provide anecdotes and vignettes that illuminate infants' and toddlers' amazing social competencies and offer suggestions for how teachers can best partner with families to nurture infants and toddlers as they grow. We address the ways that relationship-based care extends beyond the infant–toddler room and into the entire childcare community through center policies and practices that support relationship-based care.

In Chapter 5, "The Complex Role of Infant–Toddler Professionals: Care, Love, Diversity, and Identities," we delve more deeply into the multiple and complex roles of infant–toddler professionals in childcare. We share both the historical context and more current ways of thinking about the intersections among care, education, and love as integral and equally important aspects of infant–toddler professional practice. We emphasize the value and significance of reflection as a tool for reconceptualizing practice, as caregivers negotiate tensions among their own cultural and personal beliefs, professional knowledge, and the perspectives and experiences of diverse children and families.

In Chapter 6, "Becoming an Infant–Toddler Teacher: Ways of Thinking and Ways of Being," we articulate the importance of relationship-focused professional preparation as a vehicle for introducing infant–toddler teachers to enactments of high-quality, responsive care. We discuss the value of primary caregiving as an essential framework for promoting responsive care, and the ways it can benefit children, teachers, and families. We emphasize the importance of field-based practicum experiences for preservice and in-service early childhood teachers, allowing time and space to learn the meaning of relationships with infants and toddlers through direct practice. This chapter also provides suggestions for the ways that mentoring and support for infant–toddler caregivers might unfold during teacher preparation and throughout their teaching lives.

Chapter 7, "Constellations of Care: Building Caring Infant–Toddler Communities," speaks to the importance of administrative and policy supports that make an essential contribution to providing quality, responsive infant–toddler childcare. We describe what we call "constellations of caring" as a means of providing a safe and nurturing community for children, families, and professionals that goes beyond what happens in the teaching and learning context of an infant–toddler room. We discuss the ways that infusing an ethic of care into every aspect of infant–toddler childcare serves to nurture well-being in all members of the childcare community.

Chapter 8, "Enduring Reflections for the Field of Infant–Toddler Care and Education," offers further contemplations for enriching our understandings and practices in infant–toddler childcare. We envision a future where all infants and toddlers can claim their right to responsive and loving care; infant–toddler teachers can be prepared, respected, and supported for the essential and complex role they play in children's and families futures; and infant–toddler childcare can become a home for fostering community and subjective well-being for all those involved. We return to the principles articulated in Chapter 1 to frame our visions for the future.

Each of the chapters in Parts I and II concludes with a series of questions for further thought and discussion. Please also use these questions as catalysts for reflection.

CHAPTER SUMMARY

As described in our introductory remarks, we set out in this book to illuminate what we have learned through practice and research about providing quality, responsive, relationship-based childcare for infants, toddlers, and families. Guided by a set of principles that have informed our practice as both infant–toddler practitioners and teacher educators, we see essential elements of quality infant–toddler childcare embedded in everyday practice. In this introductory chapter, we have presented an image of the child as a social and emotional being who is innately competent and motivated to learn. We have highlighted the role of the caregiver as knowledgeable, responsive, supportive, and reflective. We have conceptualized the infant–toddler childcare center as a caring community that welcomes diverse children, families, and professionals as interconnected members in early care and education. Finally, we have provided a brief introduction to how these components of quality relationship-based childcare will be elaborated in the chapters that follow.

Part I

DISTINCTIVE INFANT–TODDLER SOCIAL ENCOUNTERS IN CHILDCARE

CHAPTER 2

Infant–Toddler Play as an Essential Component of Early Learning and Development

Julia, 15 months, is on the floor trying to stack up several colorful blocks, but they keep falling down. Andy, 11 months, crawls toward her, scoots next to her, and watches. Julia continues to try to place one block on top of another, but her construction falls down once again and the blocks spread on the floor. Andy reaches for one of the blocks and picks it up. He puts it in his mouth, but soon looks at Julia and extends his hand holding the block. She accepts the offer, takes the block, and adds it to her stack, trying one more time.

In this chapter we will elaborate on infant–toddler play, unfolding the definition of play during infancy and highlighting the natural way of learning and developing through play using anecdotal observations. The chapter will illustrate how responsive care within a relationship-based pedagogy is the key to developing appropriate play experiences with infants and toddlers, as caregivers are in tune with babies' needs and interests. In this framework, infants and toddlers playfully interact with each other and develop their own play experiences. Moreover, responsive caregivers support children's play through playful interactions, using a variety of materials/toys and planning activities in a flexible environment to promote children's exploration and agency. Thus, a framework of play practices will be presented with examples from praxis and vignettes, and consideration of different types of learners, while making connections with their impact on children's learning and development. Finally, we will show how infant–toddler play observation and documentation is a vital tool for caregivers to scaffold children's play endeavors.

INFANTS' AND TODDLERS' WAYS OF LEARNING

Babies are born with the predisposition and motivation to learn; early on, infants and toddlers exhibit their potentialities and capabilities in exploring their world and taking an active role in their learning (Brock & Jarvis,

2019). We acknowledge that different babies learn in different ways, but we are choosing to describe the processes that illuminate babies as active learners who intuitively, at first, engage in interactions and then with purposeful action develop their own play activities.

Action, Participation, and Interaction

Infants and toddlers in their daily caring environment show interest and become actively engaged in activities, which are either planned by their caregivers or they develop themselves, using the toys and materials around them. They participate in free play with other children and/or adults, and through these playful interactions they begin to develop their skills in all areas of learning. At the same time, they find it fun and interesting to participate in adult- or peer-led playful interactions, such as hide-and-seek games or peek-a-boo games, which give them a sense of belonging to a group.

Observation, Copying/Imitating, and Repetition

Infants and toddlers take their time in observing others, peers and/or adults, and then try to copy the actions or behaviors they have observed. When this imitation is fun, or when they receive positive reactions from peers and/or adults, they repeat the actions or behaviors with pride and joy. This repetition provides them with opportunities to expand their understanding of the activity, acknowledge the interaction, and perfect their skills (Wittmer, 2012).

> *Elly and Nick, 18 and 20 months, play with the building material (connecting plastic pipes) without interacting with each other while their caregiver, Yona, observes them. Yona then moves to their table and plays with the toys herself, connecting the pipes with no verbal interaction with the children. Elly watches Yona intensely, utters the word "wow," and then tries to put her own pieces together. Elly, after observing Yona, makes a triangle with the tubes and puts it on her wrist. Elly says, "What I do? I make bracelet." Yona tells Elly she did a great job and that what she made is very beautiful. Elly shakes the bracelet with pride and then proceeds to make other bracelets.*

In this scenario, Elly observes her caregiver Yona's constructing process and copies some of her actions, thus being able to use the materials to create a bracelet, as she proudly states.

Exploration, Experimentation, and Discovery

Infants and toddlers explore their surroundings using their whole bodies. They experiment with their abilities, using materials and toys they find in their environment; this experimentation leads them to discover either things/ actions they can do themselves or concepts that help them understand the world around them. Through these processes they acquire new knowledge and develop their skills further. Some children do this naturally, while others need guidance and support, so we must be available for them, prepared to guide them.

Play during infancy is a state of being; infants and toddlers use their bodies and minds to explore and learn about the world. They also use their senses as important tools to experiment with their surroundings and test their abilities. Infants and toddlers explore their environment, learn about it, and test and develop their knowledge and skills through action, active engagement, and interaction. All of their behaviors are a form of play, and when they play, they learn, so play clearly constitutes an important way for them to develop (Bruce, 2017). Goldschmied and Jackson (2004) talk about heuristic play, which refers to the provision of everyday objects (e.g., duster, pans, pots, sponge) that children can naturally investigate to discover their properties. This type of play clearly describes how infants and toddlers explore the objects and toys around them and exhibit their thought processes. When considering infant and toddler play, we think of the multiple opportunities we can offer children to explore, develop skills, and learn concepts within a relationship-based context.

As we show in this book, a relationship-based context is the framework that theorizes our work with infants and toddlers. Any infant and toddler setting that respects babies also values the development of relationships, as they are the basis on which children feel safe and allow themselves to become active members of a group (Recchia, 2012). Infant and toddler settings that value relationships within a play environment provide children the tools they need to successfully develop and learn. Children most often participate in play and explore their world when they feel comfortable with the people close to them, and when their play environment feels safe for exploration.

INFANTS' AND TODDLERS' PLAY EXPERIENCES

Infants and toddlers use the same processes they employ in learning when involved in play activity, as the two are hardly separated; playing is a way that children use to learn (Lillemyr, 2009). As infants and toddlers participate in play experiences with determined and constant effort, they try to do things or act upon toys and objects in particular ways, no matter how challenging the experiences might be. Insisting on and repeating their actions is their way of being actively engaged in play. They are challenged to try and aim to explore, and once they put their mind to something, they attempt to succeed in it, but sometimes this is not an easy process because they may fail. Smilansky, Parten, and Piaget have categorized children's play in ways that focus on their distinct abilities, social, emotional, or cognitive. We strongly support that each child is unique and has their own pace of development, their own ways of learning, but categorizing play provides us with a framework through which we can view a child's journey in play experiences.

So, we can refer to exploratory play, at the onset of infants' play experiences, during which children explore their environment with their body and senses. They can be involved in solitary play exploring toys/objects, and at other times may share their play with their caregivers. Play experiences relate to the child's abilities, interests, and needs, as well as the provision of materials/toys along with supportive caregivers around them. Infants and toddlers are often viewed as lonely players because they play on their own (solitary play) and then are involved in parallel play, during which they explore different objects and toys while being next to their peers, without necessarily communicating with them. They are sharing the same space and toys but initially may not be interacting to create a play experience together.

Play development is expressed uniquely at different points of a child's life, and it is important to view each moment as valuable, in order to respond to their needs and provide them with opportunities to develop the diverse skills that each form of play enhances (Gordon Biddle et al., 2014; Sheridan, 2009). We agree with Singer and de Haan (2007), who state that children are "active learners . . . relational beings . . . who . . . co-construct shared meanings and togetherness" (pp. 311–314). Infants and toddlers demonstrate the following play engagements: (1) play with toys (exploration of objects); (2) play with others (peers and caregivers); (3) pretend play/role-play; and (4) constructive play, such as block play, which will be elaborated below.

Play With Toys: Exploration of Objects

Young infants use their mouths to taste and explore items in their environment, such as toys or other objects. Once they develop the skill of grasping, they grasp objects to place them in their mouth, as this is their way of learning more about those objects and what they can do. When they become mobile, they use objects, trying to see what they can do with them. They enjoy exploring the function of toys and experimenting with their cause-and-effect actions (Hughes, 2010). When they move to toddlerhood, they are even more independent and mobile, so objects such as push toys or tricycles are used with joy and excitement. The following vignette is an example of active play in which a toddler exhibits large motor skills while involved in climbing a slide.

> *Angelina, 17 months, walks toward the slide. She climbs up the steps one at a time, without holding onto the side. Once she reaches the top, she sits down,*

places each hand on the side handles, and slides with great ease. While sliding, she laughs and shows excitement. She repeats the process three times.

Open-ended toys and materials that have multiple uses support children's exploration and experimentation, providing them with diverse opportunities to discover what they can do and how to use these toys, while developing skills and learning concepts. The use of toys and materials in children's play motivates their play engagement and responds to their abilities and needs. Infants exhibit great excitement in exploring a large cardboard box while at the same time learning about spatial concepts; they place toys inside the box, they move the box around, they use their whole body to go inside the box—the potentialities of this material are great. Through focused choices of materials and toys, development and learning can be playfully enhanced (Hughes, 2010; Løkken, 2000).

Toddlers' use of toys enriches their play behaviors and makes them more mature players. They use objects to add to their roles or to expand their scenarios, or they use objects to create their own games, which they may share with peers or caregivers. In considering *all* children, we must ensure they have enough time and space to explore the potential of toys/materials provided, and to begin to understand their functionality. Additionally, "size, density, organisation and thematic arrangement are [always important] considerations with play materials" (Movahedazarhouligh, 2018, p. 592).

Anna, 10 months, is on the floor, with big fluffy pillows on either side because she is not completely balanced in a sitting position. A plastic dolphin is in front of her. She observes the dolphin for a long time and attempts to reach it by stretching her body in front. She then flips over and begins to cry. Her caregiver helps her sit up again. After a while, Anna attempts again and reaches for the dolphin with her left hand. She manages to grasp the dolphin but then falls on her back. She whines and puts the dolphin figure in her mouth.

This scenario provides an example of an infant who needs time to explore materials around her, and who might make several unsuccessful attempts before she manages to do what she aims to do. We acknowledge and respect this, taking care to provide children enough time and space for them to act at their own pace.

Infants and toddlers are like scientists who experiment, employ trial and error, and repeat certain actions in order to reach their goal. For infants, though, sometimes these actions and their outcomes are planned and focused, while at other times they are random. Infants and toddlers are seen to aim toward a specific action with specific toys, for example, to place a particular shaped block in a sorting box. They attempt to do so several times until they succeed, but there are times that while trying to fit the block in the box, they accidentally uncover the box and then a new goal is set—one that involves emptying and refilling the box. We thus acknowledge that during play children might have specific goals but that these are fluid and relate to how the experience unfolds.

Play With Others (Peers and Caregivers)

Infant–caregiver play is more common in under-2s, where the caregiver responds or initiates play interactions, such as a game of peek-a-boo. The caregiver responds to the child's cues, and an interactive game begins; "Interactions are relational and reciprocal" (Wittmer, 2012, p. 18). Infants and caregivers follow each other's lead, and they unfold playful interaction, creating a safe space for children to explore (Andrews, 2012).

> *Alice, 6 months, is in her bouncy chair. Her caregiver is sitting in front of her and is blowing bubbles up in the air in front of Alice and saying, "Wow! Look, Alice, how many bubbles, and how high they go! Oh, look some are coming toward you! Do you want to touch them?!" Alice keeps her eyes on one bubble, which is right in front of her. When the bubble bursts, she moves her eyes toward another one. She smiles and slowly stretches both of her hands in front of her body, trying to touch the bubbles while making squeaking sounds.*

This vignette provides a clear example of infant–caregiver interaction. Alice and her caregiver share a playful experience in which the caregiver leads the activity and Alice actively follows with her body, showing signs of joy.

Research shows how, early on, infants not only share social interactions with caregivers but also with peers, who they see as a reflection of themselves (Meltzoff, 2010). They specifically show interest in peers of the same age, with whom they share the same learning context. At first, they smile at each other, vocalize, and then they begin to touch and imitate each other's play behavior (Trevarthen, 2003). During toddlerhood, physical contact often occurs as toddlers give and take objects/toys and communicate within and about their play context (Degotardi & Pearson, 2014).

> *Nick and Julie, 26 months, are playing in the kitchen area. Julie takes a spoon and a fork from a drawer. She then takes a baby doll, sits on the chair, and begins to pretend to feed her, using the spoon. Nick watches Julie, and then opens another kitchen drawer, takes out a bottle, and hands it to Julie, saying "milk."*

In this vignette, the two toddlers share a pretend play interaction. Julie exhibits pretend play behaviors in using specific materials to feed a baby doll, while Nick attempts to extend their play scenario using both materials and language. Nick's action is more functional, as the bottle of milk is better related to the feeding of a baby. The two toddlers appear to support one another in their play.

Infant–Toddler Play as an Essential Component of Early Learning and Development 19

This kind of social interaction, however, is not an easy process for some infants or toddlers due to lack of language or social cues. One example might be for a child on the autistic spectrum who has difficulty reading others' social responses. Infants and toddlers might need the support of caregivers or peers in the form of gestures, words, and play invitation actions in order to begin to develop these social interaction behaviors in their play (Movahedazarhouligh, 2018, p. 592). Through the exploration of themselves, others, and the world, they can participate in playful actions during which they develop or enhance particular skills. Wittmer (2012) comments on "how concerned, helpful, empathetic, cooperative and friendly" (p. 16) infants and toddlers can be. They tend to have both successful and unsuccessful attempts in play, and it is crucial that they have these opportunities to learn to cope with failures and to appreciate successes, both of which are important for their self-confidence and motivation to learn.

Pretend Play/Role-Play

Infants observe the adults around them and imitate their actions, thus beginning to role-play. They pretend to be on the phone by placing a toy phone on their ear, or hold the TV remote control, pretending to turn the TV on. Such behaviors exhibit their ability to enact a play episode. Toddlers become more capable in role-play as they pretend to be enacting more elaborated actions. For example, they might pretend to be on the phone, holding a toy phone and using language to talk to someone. Or they might pretend they are feeding a doll in the kitchen area, using materials and toys while interacting with another toddler (see vignette below with Christine and Alexandros).

We also know that babies enjoy other babies and adults even more than they enjoy toys or objects, and that peer play is enhanced around the age of 2 years. Toddlers show interest in pretend play with their peers and have the abilities to joyfully participate in it. In her research, Morrissey (2014) has shown that "with supportive play partners and appropriate play materials, infants and toddlers can quite rapidly acquire the full repertoire of the symbolic cognitive processes that underlie pretend play, and within months become independent players" (p. 208).

> *Christine, 30 months, places a baby doll in the stroller and takes her around the classroom. Alexandros (28 months old) follows her and suddenly says "poop! the baby pooped." Christine looks at Alexandros and says, "let's change her diaper." They move to another area of the classroom, and Christine removes the baby's clothes. Alexandros says, "No forget cream!" Christine pretends to put on cream and says "finish!" They place the doll back in the stroller and continue their classroom stroll.*

Christine and Alexandros exhibit complex pretend play behaviors, taking on the domestic roles of a mom and dad, although these are not expressed. Their actions show the evolvement of a scenario with specific episodes in reference to caring for an infant. They use both materials and language to develop their scenario, while accepting each other's offers, as expected in pretend play.

Although infants have similar basic needs in development and learning, they are unique beings who need to be considered within their own pace of development and their temperament, personality, and way of learning. Not all infants and toddlers experience pretend play in the same manner; some might need more realistic objects of an appropriate size in order to be able to effectively use them, and they might enjoy following an adult or a peer in their play involvement. In some cases, adults can best support particular infants and toddlers in participating in role enactment by simplifying the play actions (Perino & Besio, 2017).

Ellie, 32 months, enjoys playing with dolls, but her play is repetitive, she does not share her toys with others, and she does not have a scenario. Marie, Ellie's caregiver, joins in as a mother and pretends to hold another baby doll. Marie uses language to show that she is taking care of her baby and invites Ellie to do the same. After a couple of days, Marie decides to join in again and pretend that her baby is hungry by making crying noises; she uses toys, a spoon and a bowl, to feed her baby. Ellie watches Marie and asks for a spoon herself. They both pretend to feed their baby. In a week's time, Marie notices that Ellie is pretending to feed the doll. She invites Peter, 33 months, to join in by giving him a stroller and a baby doll, explaining the baby needs to go for a stroll. Then Ellie says "stroll," and Marie provides her with a stroller as well. Marie then invites the children to take their babies on a stroll.

This scenario shows how a caregiver gradually develops a toddler's role-play through supporting her scenario and peer interaction.

Constructive Play-Block Play

Infants and toddlers are often involved in playing with blocks (wooden or plastic bricks); they find them interesting materials with which to experiment. The potentialities of blocks and other similar constructive play toys (e.g., Legos or bristle blocks) motivate infants and toddlers to use them in different ways; they put them in their mouth, bang them on the floor, move them around, put them next to each other forming lines, stack them on top of each other, create patterns, and attempt to build (e.g., a tower or a bridge).

Constructive play for infants and toddlers begins with exploration, transferring blocks in different areas, and moves to simple building and enclosed structures (Loizou, 2019). Such experiences are closely related to infants' and toddlers' fine motor skills (i.e., use, coordination, and control of small muscles) as well as cognitive skills such as observing, grouping, testing, and experimenting for problem solving (Loizou, 2021). So, "to build something a child needs not only to be able to manipulate the components, but also to be able to visualize and plan the object in her head" (Sheridan, 2006, p. 9). As shown in the chapter's opening anecdote, infants can be persistent in trying to build a tower, as this can be a fun and challenging play activity.

Peer-Play Interactions

In unfolding peer-play interactions, it is important to talk about shared meanings, imitation, and friendship, as these are crucial for the quality of the play interactions. Valuing relationships and considering them the most important context through which infants and toddlers experience learning, we especially focus on peer-play interactions. By doing so, we aim to unfold the many ways in which infants and toddlers exchange and enrich each other's play experiences.

Van Oers and Hännikäinen (2001) discuss "togetherness" as a way infants and toddlers come together in a childcare setting, exhibiting joint social activity contextualized through play. Children who experience the same routines daily, share the same space and toys, as well as the caring of specific caregivers, develop caring feelings for their peers. In their daily context, infants and toddlers learn to interact and exchange social playful interactions as a way to show their curiosity, express their feelings, and convey their needs. In this context, Lindahl and Pramling Samuelsson (2002), along with Rutanen (2007), show through their studies how toddlers, when involved in play, imitate each other's actions while also exhibiting unique ways of acting. Through emergent or purposeful playful interactions, infants and toddlers exhibit "collective and individual learning."

Research highlights infant and toddler interactions with their peers, and we have long seen in baby rooms how babies look, smile, vocalize, and touch each other in an attempt to communicate. Infants and toddlers show great interest in each other and use multiple subtle, as well as not so subtle, ways to express their needs and ability for social encounters. Shin (2012) explains how infants under 2 years of age use "communicative gestures; gaze following, eye contact, joint attention and pointing" (p. 312) when involved in social play. Also, studies on toddler friendships (Engdahl, 2012; Greve, 2009) show how children who are friends find playful ways to interact and greet each other in childcare, using various ways, verbally or physically or through gaze, to invite them to play.

Mario and Nicolas, both 15 months, run from one end of the classroom to the other, squealing with joy. Mario sits on the floor with his back touching the door of the classroom, and immediately Nicolas imitates. Nicolas moves his body closer to Mario, and they look at each other. They babble and smile while moving their legs up and down. Mario gets up, waits, looks at Nicolas, and runs away. Nicolas gets up and runs after Mario.

Babies as relational beings strive to find ways to interact and exchange experiences with their peers. In these exchanges, they imitate each other, they share the meaning of the experience and, living it together, they develop a sense of togetherness, as exemplified in the anecdote above. Social peer interactions can be positive, especially when infants and toddlers share play materials and ideas, and the context of play provides the space for joint attention, joy, and excitement, as we see with Mario and Nicolas. That said, in some instances, peer interaction and communication is not so successful, as shown in the following vignette.

Jane, 24 months, is playing in the kitchen area. She takes some spoons and forks and places them in the sink to wash. Lily, 26 months, is holding a bowl; she approaches Jane, says "spoon" and takes a spoon from the sink. She then begins to pretend to eat from the bowl, using the spoon. Jane approaches, extends her hand, and pulls the spoon from Lily's hands. Lily responds by bringing her mouth closer to Jane's hand, ready to bite her. The caregiver observing their interaction intervenes, extending her hand in front of Lily's mouth.

This vignette shows how infants and toddlers can be sharing play experiences that might end unsuccessfully. In the realm of relationship-based care, interaction with others in a play context is crucial regardless of its outcome because it provides important opportunities for social learning.

INFANT–TODDLER PLAY PRACTICES AND THE CAREGIVER ROLE

Recchia and Fincham (2019) discuss how infant–toddler curriculum draws from infants' and toddlers' day-to-day experiences and their overall development and learning processes, while also considering the constant changes in their developing skills and abilities (Bergen et al., 2009). It is important to highlight the dualistic role of caregivers: in caring, developing responsive relationships with children; and in education, consciously considering and planning for their learning and development. In *Enhancing Brain Development in Infants and Young Children*, Bergen, Lee, DiCarlo, and Burnett (2020) highlight how early care can have a positive impact on children's brain development and that caregivers are already enacting "brain enhancing curricular practices" (p. 3). They denote the importance of play for infants and toddlers in developing symbolic, problem-solving, communication, and negotiation skills. Thus in conceptualizing infants' and toddlers' optimal progress, we sustain play as a vital learning context because it takes place within meaningful and responsive interactive relationships with caregivers. But, as Recchia (2016) points out, "teaching in this way requires a great deal of consciousness and intellectual effort for the teachers" (p. 92).

Infant and toddler caregivers draw from specific ways of organizing learning and teaching practices to unfold play experiences for children. Some early childhood literature differentiates between teacher-initiated and child-centered teaching approaches. These dichotomies have been questioned by Jung and Recchia (2013) and by Shin and Partyka (2017), who propose different approaches. Specifically, Jung and Recchia (2013) refer to scaffolding approaches and see caregivers as "facilitators and scaffolders" (p. 831) who engage in children's play to support it and to validate their learning. They also highlight "individualized scaffolding" (p. 846) as crucial in responding to each infant separately and more effectively. Shin and Partyka (2017) support the use of teacher-initiated play activities, as well as child-initiated play, to best respond to all infants' and toddlers' needs and learning styles. Shin and Partyka suggest that best practice does not necessarily distinguish teacher-directed from child-initiated ways of organizing learning. Rather, what is most important is to develop relationships that will support meaningful ways of interacting, and to provide play opportunities that enhance the way children learn and develop. Extending on this, Recchia and Shin (2012) point out the importance of synchronous teacher–child connections on which teaching needs to be based.

Acknowledging the above-mentioned planning elements for infants' and toddlers' learning and development, Loizou and Demetriou (2019) examined ways of organizing learning experiences through a playful context. These include routines, purposeful play intervention, structured play, and quiet-time observation. Before looking more closely at each of these four elements, we want to emphasize that while providing effective learning experiences is always crucial, our top priority is to be flexible and respectful of the children. We also want to offer a word of caution about potential intrusion through structuring of children's experiences and learning. What we propose provides caregivers a mapping of ways to work with infants and toddlers, unfolding the diversity of pedagogic potential in the work that can be done with young children.

Routines

Routines are the actions that take place daily involving the care of infants and toddlers, such as feeding and diaper changing. Such actions can be used to provide children with ample opportunities for learning (Gonzalez-Mena & Eyer, 2007). They are very important for infants and toddlers because they provide the consistency they need to feel comfortable and at ease, as well the sense that they are being cared for and their needs are being met. Infants and toddlers do not differentiate their behavior based on context, thus during routines they act playfully and explore every experience as play (Degotardi, 2010). They play with the diaper or the cream when changing a diaper; they play with their food when eating with their peers around a table. They find ways to use the materials involved in routines in a playful way, and many times routines turn into play activities. For example, when a toddler is toilet trained and uses the bathroom, she can turn the washing of her hands into a play activity and spend more time exploring the water until being asked by her caregiver to return to what she was doing.

During free play, infants and toddlers explore their environment freely and engage in activities based on their interests, strengths, and needs. They explore materials and toys and indirectly exercise their skills and begin to learn specific concepts. Caregivers are nearby to observe and support children when necessary. They can be responsive to children by using language to describe their actions, or they can provide children with new or more toys and materials in order to promote experimentation.

Purposeful Playful Intervention

"Purposeful playful intervention refers to the teacher's playful actions after observing the infants during their daily activities (e.g., free play, routines) and assessing the moment as a learning opportunity—a moment when the child can practice a skill or learn a concept" (Loizou & Demetriou, 2019, p. 5). It is recognized that nearly everything can be play and playful for infants and toddlers, and that the caregiver is available for every child. At the same time, the caregiver offers play opportunities using toys, materials, and other children. Moreover, the caregiver makes conscious interventions after observing the children in order to support them within their play context. They engage in infant–toddler play interactions during which they improvise based on the children's current needs (e.g., begin a peek-a-boo game or put on music and dance with the children). During most play interactions with children, caregivers provide the necessary space for children to take the lead, engaging only when invited or as needed.

For example, after observing a child's frustration in trying to place puzzle pieces, a caregiver can playfully model how to properly do a puzzle. Or, if a child is playing with blocks, the caregiver may model how to place blocks one on top of another, or demonstrate how to use a shape-sorting box. Caregivers' play interventions strive to support children's overall development, including cognitive, motor, linguistic, and socioemotional. When caregivers consider purposeful playful intervention, they act as if following an emergent curriculum, following the children's lead. In doing so, their pedagogic actions are balanced so that they avoid acting "too much" (intrusion) or "too little" (missing opportunities), either of which can interfere with children's opportunities for learning through play.

Structured Play

"Structured play refers to goal-oriented play which caregivers have planned beforehand, with specific learning goals and previously prepared materials" (Loizou & Demetriou, 2019, p. 5). Structured play can involve activities that refer to creative play (i.e., music or art play), where the caregiver provides the materials and initiates the play activity, inviting children to participate. The expectation is for the children to engage in these playful activities in different ways, guided by caregivers, for as long as they like. Caregivers are there to support children's interactions among themselves as well as their exploration of materials. Of course, such play is important for *all* children, including those who lack specific experiences or "need a gentle push to try new things" (Shin & Partyka, 2017, p. 139). Moreover, in the case of a child with intellectual disabilities, this experience will provide the support needed for the child to undergo a process effectively, to focus, and perhaps to aim at a product (e.g., playing with emotion cards or puzzles with emotions and expressing those), a process they might not be able to do on their own. Also, structured play is a planned way that caregivers use to focus on promoting infants and toddlers to play together as a group. The planning of a group play activity is an opportunity to promote interaction among children and to develop a community of players, and thus learners.

> The caregiver, wearing a hat (pretending to be a train driver), says, "Time to play! Who is ready to play, sing, and dance? If you are, come close!" Kate, 20 months; Chris, 23 months; and Peter, 19 months, run with joy toward their caregiver, Ali. Ali holds a scarf, waves it, and says, "Remember our story about the train? Let's all create our own train to travel far away. I can be the driver." Ali then invites the children to stand in a line, touching each other on the shoulder, and giving them the scarf to hold with one of their hands. Holding the edge of the scarf, Ali starts walking, encouraging the children to follow her, while singing the train song: "Our train is ready to go, choo-choo the train goes, choo-choo the train passes . . ." Ali then invites Chris to be the driver and gives Chris the hat, gesturing for her to move first in line. They continue singing the song while moving around the classroom. Peter decides to let go of the scarf and watches them all, smiling. They repeat the process once or twice, with Ali encouraging other children to be the train driver.

Taking into consideration the children's previous experience, that of reading a book about a train, the caregiver planned and executed a structured movement activity that invited children to participate. They accepted her invitation and participated in moving and singing along with their peers. There was no pressure to participate; if a child preferred only to observe, this was not a problem.

Quiet-Time Observation

Quiet-time observation is a way for caregivers to communicate nonverbally with the children. In essence, the caregiver quietly observes the children while they are playing either on their own or along with each other. During quiet-time observation, the caregiver becomes a secure base for infants and toddlers to playfully explore their environment. When necessary, with the use of facial expressions and subtle movements, the caregiver responds to children's play cues and sustains their play experience (Hammond, 2009; Tortora, 2011). Through this practice, caregivers provide infants and toddlers with the space and time they need to explore their surroundings and play independently.

> *Alex, 7 months, is laying with his belly down on a mat, next to Ariana, 9 months. The caregiver is on the floor close to them. Alex and Ariana both move their hands, trying to reach a cloth book in front of them. Alex places his hands on the mat, folds his fingers, and creates a fist, extending his body and face to examine the picture book. Ariana extends her feet, giving herself a push forward to reach the book with her palms open on the mat. The caregiver observes the children and their actions from a close distance. She then moves the book a little further from the children. Alex moves his feet back and forth more intensely while extending his hands. Ariana changes her position; she uses her knees and hands to push her body forward to reach the book, and she succeeds. She grasps one page with her right hand while expressing sounds of excitement. The caregiver looks at her and smiles. Alex is still trying; after a while, he extends his body and head and pushes his feet, moving closer to the book. He extends his right hand, opens his palm, and with his fingers pulls the book close to him.*

This vignette involving quiet-time observation illustrates how caregivers can develop a richer and deeper understanding of infants' and toddlers' capabilities and personality. Such information can help caregivers appreciate infants as learners and be more effective in supporting their learning and development. This type of practice can be difficult for caregivers who are "high energy" or feel that true teachers are only really teaching when they actively participate in children's play through talking or action. Loizou and Recchia (2018) explored how teachers new to working with infants reconceptualized their caregiving role. The teachers commented on how they "had to restrain themselves and felt uncomfortable" (p. 98) during quiet-time observation. Viewing themselves via video and further analyzing their actions, however, they were able to realize that through this specific practice they allowed space for children to initiate and invite them into their own play world, rather than the children following their lead.

Caregivers' playful endeavors through routines, emergent or structured play activities, and free play provide a balance of interactions responding to children's individual needs while at the same time ensuring learning and development. To best respond to the individual needs of children, caregivers must be flexible and playful, taking advantage of all available learning opportunities. They must make conscious, well-thought-out decisions, based on their observations, on how to act and engage with infants and toddlers. Loizou (2017) discusses different play typologies for preschoolers, but her work relates as much to infants and toddlers, who also experience play opportunities in unique ways based on their abilities. Thus, "individual scaffolding," as proposed by Jung and Recchia (2013), is a key method to be incorporated by caregivers because it acknowledges the individual needs and potentialities of children and builds space to effectively support their learning and development. Furthermore, drawing from Recchia and Shin's (2012) study on the level of synchrony between caregivers' and infants' social interactions, it is argued that being in sync with infants and toddlers, in all of the strategies just discussed—routines, structured play, purposeful playful intervention, quiet-time observation—is a critical component in responsive quality play interactions.

In order to be responsive to all children, "physical, social and temporal modifications" (Rausch et al., 2021, p. 17) must be considered by caregivers when designing a caring learning environment. "Alterations to the environment . . . planned interactions among children . . . and adjustments in timing of routines and activities" (p. 17) exhibit the quality and responsive caregiving that is considered inclusive of all infants and toddlers. Additionally, Shin and Partyka (2017) highlight that caregivers must consider infants and toddlers both individually and as a group. It is evident that balance is key to appropriate care for infants and toddlers, allowing caregivers to plan and implement play activities for and with *all* children.

Observation, Documentation, and Reflection

For caregivers to be successful in creating meaningful and learning-full experiences for infants and toddlers, it is important that they systematically observe and document children's interactions and actions during play. These observations need to be as detailed as possible, in order to record all the important information entailed in the infants' and toddlers' play experiences (Page et al., 2013). For this to happen, caregivers must have set routines for how and when observation can take place. Some caregivers use a recording system, noting on the spot unique play actions they observe; others have a set time of day to record what they have observed when interacting with children. The early childhood education literature provides multiple methods for caregivers to employ when observing play (e.g., narratives, checklists, sociograms, event sampling) (Andrews, 2012). A caregiver needs to consider good planning along with the purpose of the observation so that it can be most effective.

Observation during play allows caregivers to record children's learning and development, along with their play skills. Also, play observation provides caregivers a peek into infants' and toddlers' play interests—preferred toys, materials, space, play partners, play activity choices, and more. With this information, caregivers can best plan for a play-oriented curriculum, while also carefully considering their involvement during play time. As Formosinho (2016) suggests, pedagogic documentation reveals learning and teaching in the making. Thus, observation and documentation of infants' and toddlers' play provides caregivers information on which they can base their planning and play scaffolding. Moreover, it is important to include reflection, both while observing and while interpreting play documentation, as reflection allows for deeper analysis of children's play actions, as well as one's own practice (Hughes, 2001).

In the textbox below we include a sample list of questions that can be used by caregivers to reflect on the play observations and documentation they enact, so as to draw the necessary information to best provide for infants and toddlers, both individually and as a group. Observation, documentation, and reflection are crucial to any educator's practice, and equally so for infant–toddler caregivers. Quality relationship-based and responsive care is based on observation, documentation, and reflection, as these actions respect infants' and toddlers' genuine needs and value their abilities.

SAMPLE OBSERVATION QUESTIONS

- How much time does the child spend in using the sorting box? How does the child play with the sorting box?
- What feelings does the child express when using a baby doll?
- Can the child initiate play interaction with peers? How does the child do this?
- Does the child respond to caregivers' and/or peers' play invitations?
- How does the child express ideas during a group play activity with peers? Does the child use language, movement, touching, imitation, pushing?
- Can the child share space when on the floor and playing with a toy?
- How does the child react after placing five blocks on top of each other?

DISCUSSION QUESTIONS

1. What role does play have in your life?
2. What can you learn about an infant or a toddler when employing quiet-time observation during play? What can you learn about yourself as a caregiver?
3. How do you react when you see an infant using a toy in other than its expected way of use?
4. Thinking about your practice, how do you support infants' and toddlers' play? What is the role of time and space in nurturing play experiences?
5. How would you react when toddlers don't participate in the fun creative play activities you plan?

CHAPTER 3

Friendships Among Infant–Toddler Peers

Myla, 13 months, arrives at the classroom with her dad in the morning. Looking at the door, the caregiver, Vanessa, says to Emily, 14 months, "Someone's at the door." Emily turns her body toward the door, saying, "Myla. Myla." Emily then runs quickly to the door, calling Myla. Vanessa excitedly responds, "Myla is here. She's here. She's here," throwing her arms in the air. Emily grabs the door (an approximately 18-inch-tall room divider door), shaking it and calling Myla's name continuously in a loud and excited voice. Myla enters the room and walks around. Emily greets Myla with a hug and kisses. Emily then follows Myla, calling her name loudly. Myla sits on the floor, and Emily sits down right in front of her. Facing Myla, Emily says, "Hi." Myla also says "Hi" to Emily, and they both laugh. Emily gives Myla a big hug and holds her tightly, saying her name repeatedly.

In this anecdote, Emily exhibits a distinct interest in her peer, Myla. When Myla arrives at the center, Emily cannot stop saying Myla's name, following her around, and hugging her. Emily and Myla greet each other and share affection and closeness. Infants, as portrayed here, do demonstrate early friendship. This anecdote showing joyful reciprocal affection expressed toward preferred friends raises the question of whether this early friendship experience is exceptional. Can infants and toddlers have friends?

We know that early friendship experiences can substantially contribute to the development and learning of young children, and that they play a unique and crucial role in early social experience (Hartup, 1996). Infants and toddlers in childcare can and do form special bonds with particular peers that enhance their social and emotional lives. Their reciprocal connections are reflected in both their shared enjoyment of rituals and play and their empathic responses to one another in times of stress. Yet, friendships among infants and toddlers and their social implications have not been extensively explored (Degotardi & Pearson, 2009; Musatti et al., 2017; Wittmer, 2008). Our aim in this chapter is to highlight social capabilities among infants and toddlers as they relate to friendship. Our extensive

30

examination of infant–toddler friendships will counter the common notions of "egocentric" and "solitary" infants and toddlers.

This chapter begins with a brief synthesis of the literature on infant–toddler friendships. Special attention is paid to the characteristics of unique friendship experiences infants and toddlers co-create and share. Next, we discuss infant–toddler friendship experiences and sociocultural context. We will examine the individual and developmental differences in infant–toddler friendships and discuss the role of conflict in the early relationship-building process. Finally, we examine how infant–toddler teachers' pedagogical decisions can either scaffold or hinder the development of friendship experiences among diverse infants and toddlers.

INFANT–TODDLER FRIENDSHIPS

We know that young children are social beings from birth. The ways that infants can engage communicatively, experience shared attention, and be in sync with adult caregivers have been beautifully documented (Dunn, 2004). During most of the 20th century, the study of infant–toddler relationships focused heavily on mother–child relationships and attachment, as parents were viewed as primarily responsible for socialization (Eckerman & Peterman, 2001; Raikes & Edwards, 2009). Friendship experiences among infants and toddlers, on the other hand, have not been extensively studied.

The dominance of Piaget's developmental theory in the 1960s might be a possible explanation for why the examination of young children's peer relationships was limited. Piaget (1932/1965) believed that young children are egocentric and unable to distinguish one's own perspective from that of others. This influential and strongly pervasive notion of infants and toddlers as egocentric affords a view of young children as cognitively inflexible and passive, focusing only on their own simple state of being. This view likely restricted the study of early social interaction and peer relationships.

Historical and Social Context

Some studies report that infants show a distinct interest in infant peers (e.g., Hay et al., 1983). Primarily conducted in lab settings, these studies showed that infants demonstrate social behaviors toward one another, including directing smiles, vocalizations, and gestures to peers, being close together in space, and looking at each other (Eckerman et al., 1975; Mueller & Vandell, 1979; Vandell et al., 1980). With age, infants exchange more complex and coordinated social interactions with peers (Eckerman et al., 1975; Mueller & Lucas, 1975), matching thoughts, feelings, and behaviors with others.

Observational studies have described infants and toddlers as socially competent, highlighting their social-communicative skills and capacity to develop early friendships (Howes, 1983; McGaha et al., 2011; Shin, 2012). Infants and toddlers can demonstrate affective, playful, caring friendships (Howes, 1983; Shin, 2010). More recent studies have been steadily challenging the popular conception of "self-centered" infants (Salamon, 2011, p. 4). We now recognize that infants have a more advanced social understanding than previously believed.

Characteristics of Friendship Experiences

This chapter begins with an essential question, "Can infants and toddlers have friends?" Infants and toddlers clearly demonstrate friendship characteristics very early. Early friendships can be characterized by strong and mutual preference, reciprocal social play, and intense affection (Hartup, 1996; Howes, 1983, 1996; Shin, 2010).

Strong and Mutual Preference. Young friends prefer their friends to other peers. They seek proximity toward each other for interaction or simply to maintain closeness (Howes, 1983, 1988; Lewis et al., 1975; Miller, 2000; Vandell et al., 1980). The two anecdotes below show how Clara and Luke demonstrated their preference to be together. In the first scenario, Clara was following Luke around and showing positive affect toward him through physical touches and kissing:

> *Clara, 12 months, crawls over to Luke, 11 months, several times and gently puts her head down on his head and shoulder. She also carefully puts her lips on his head and pats his head with her hand. She follows him as he crawls around.*

The second scenario shows Clara was very affectionate to Luke. Luke was also seeking proximity and initiating play with Clara.

> *Clara is playing with a baby doll on the floor. Clara holds up the baby and then gives a big hug to the baby doll. Clara then puts down the doll, touches its eyes and nose, and bangs it. Luke crawls by and sees Clara. Luke sits next to Clara and taps her shoulder. Luke then touches the baby doll and bangs the doll's face with Clara.*

Here, Clara and Luke exhibit mutual preference, seeking each other out particularly and deliberately. This mutual preference distinguishes friendship from other social interactions.

Reciprocal Social Play. Young friends like to be together and play together. They are playful around their preferred peers. Simply, they like to have fun with each other. Below, when a toy mirror amuses Jane, she attempts to share the joy with Anna:

Jane, 15 months, finds a small plastic mirror, puts it down on the floor, and puts her face close to the mirror to look. Jane then lifts the mirror, looks at herself, puts it down, and giggles. Jane moves close to Anna, 16 months. Jane puts the mirror very close to her nose, vocalizing, and then under Anna's chin for Anna to look. Jane takes the mirror, puts it on Anna's head, watches it falling, and hugs Anna.

Infants' and toddlers' verbal language is just emerging and developing. They thus use various nonverbal gestures and expressions to invite their preferred peers to play. As we see in the anecdote below, Liam and Abigail engage in various nonverbal communicative gestures, including gaze-following and eye contact, and experience coordinated object-focused play.

Abigail, 13 months, sits on the floor and plays with a plastic toy train. Liam, 12 months, crawls to Abigail, looks at the toy and at Abigail in turn. Liam picks up the toy train. Abigail looks at Liam, gets up, and walks over to the big green ball. Abigail starts banging the ball. Liam stops playing with the train. Liam looks at Abigail playing with the green ball. Liam smiles at Abigail when Abigail looks at him. Liam then scoots over to Abigail. Abigail and Liam bang the ball together, giggling.

Gazing is fundamental for social play. Liam carefully followed Abigail visually and figured out what was going on. Liam seemed interested in playing with Abigail, looking at the toy train and Abigail in turn. His intention, however, was not conveyed clearly. Although Abigail walked away from the scene, Liam was still interested in her and carefully observed her actions. Through gaze-following and exchange, Abigail and Liam communicated their intention to engage in social play with the green ball. Eventually, they successfully coordinate their play, banging the ball together. Positive emotion displayed at the end of the anecdote indicates how these two infant friends enjoyed playing together.

We can highlight a few critical points. First, gaze-following can be a basis for social joint play. Also, infants are more interested in social play using the same object rather than the object itself. Further, as Shin (2012) explains in her study, infant friends engage in various communicative gestures, such as gaze-following, eye contact, purposeful pointing, and joint attention.

Joint Attention. Joint attention is the ability to experience shared attention with a social partner (Mundy & Newell, 2007). Tomasello (1995) describes it as "two individuals [who] know that they are attending to something in common" (p. 106). Episodes of joint attention include various gestures, such as pointing to, making sounds, looking at, showing, or offering objects (Tomasello, 1999). When infants and toddlers interact and communicate with each other verbally or nonverbally, they have opportunities to understand others' intentions and to coordinate their attention and actions with those of their social partner (Dunham & Moore, 1995; Slomkowski & Dunn, 1996; Tomasello, 1995).

Below, Chloe and Jake interact around a breakfast cereal (Cheerios) and share a successful social interaction exchange based on social understanding and joint attention.

> *Chloe, 15 months, is sitting at the table eating Cheerios. Chloe follows Jake, 24 months, visually as she is eating. Chloe drops some of her Cheerios while eating and looks and points at them. Jake notices and picks up the Cheerios that fell on the floor. Chloe drops her Cheerios again and looks at Jake, pointing at the Cheerios. When Jake gives the Cheerios back to Chloe, she smiles at Jake.*

At first, Chloe was attentive to Jake, following him visually. She dropped some of her Cheerios with a specific purpose in mind. She pointed with imperative motives, wanting to have her Cheerios back. Jake understood Chloe's intention correctly and picked up those Cheerios from the floor for her. Chloe and Jake demonstrated how young children can observe each other's actions with interest, produce and utilize various communicative means, and successfully engage in social interaction.

It is also important to note that friends play socially using objects. Young friends engage in various types of play, such as object-exchange activities, more coordinated social play, and complementary and reciprocal play (Eckerman et al., 1989; Howes, 1983, 1985; Vandell et al., 1980). Løkken (2009) describes how toddlers involve themselves in constructing games and rituals during which they communicate with their peers using their bodies, movements, and objects.

As shown in the above vignette, Chloe and Jake developed their own social "give-and-take" game using their social communicative gestures and cereal. They observed each other's actions, comprehended the partner's intention and social motive, and engaged in complementary interactions. Infant–toddler friends engage in more successful, coordinated, and playful social interactions with each other than with other peers. Thus, social interactions and joint attention can create opportunities for the collaborative construction of knowledge and afford rich learning opportunities for young children (Brownell et al., 2006; Degotardi, 2017). In this sense, joint attention is a highly complex social-cognitive phenomenon.

Intense Affection. Young friends exhibit more positive affection through smiles, laughs, touches, vocalizations, hugs, and kisses (Lewis et al., 1975; Miller, 2000; Shin, 2010; Vandell et al., 1980). The affective nature of early friendships is what distinguishes friends from non-friend peers. Moreover, the affection that friends share should be mutual and reciprocal. Bukowski and Hoza (1989) claim that reciprocity has been used as criteria in defining

Friendships Among Infant–Toddler Peers

friendship. Infant friends express their joy and affection toward one another through their whole bodies reciprocally:

> *The children are getting ready to go out. Yasmin (caregiver) puts the children in the cart. She puts Emily, 16 months, in front of Myla, 15 months. Myla bounces her bottom, vocalizing. Yasmin says, "You are so excited." Emily suddenly gives Myla a hug. Myla accepts her hug. Then Myla cheers and claps with a smile.*

Here is another example of how Emily and Myla displayed positive, reciprocal affection toward each other, such as hugging, touching, and kissing:

> *Myla, 15 months, stands on the slide's steps. Emily, 16 months, goes up to Myla and tries to kiss her on her lips. Myla lets Emily kiss her as she sees it coming.*

Infant–toddler friends express their reciprocal or shared excitement to see each other in various ways. Hugging is an expression of affection that infant–toddler friends share to show their preference and closeness. Hugging requires mutual participation from both peers (Engdahl, 2011). Both peers should have a shared desire to establish closeness. As shown in the above anecdotes, when Emily wanted to hug and kiss Myla, Myla needed to receive these affectionate behaviors from Emily. The expression and reception of the affectionate behaviors indicate closeness and friendship.

Infant–toddler friends display not only intensive and passionate affection but also caring and prosocial behaviors toward one another (Shin, 2010).

> *Beatrice, 25 months, has a very special lovey toy that she keeps in her cubby at childcare. It is there for her when she is particularly upset or at nap time; it is only for her and doesn't have to be shared. When her friend Elizabeth, 26 months, has a hard time saying good-bye to her mommy, Beatrice reaches into her cubby and brings her special toy for Elizabeth to hold, softly patting her back as she places it in her hands.*

Infants and toddlers can understand their friends' emotional states and show empathetic behaviors, such as pats, concerned looks, and offers of comfort. Davidov and her colleagues (2013) explain that infants can turn attention toward another infant in distress, such as in response to crying. Friends are more likely to respond to a friend crying than to a non-friend, offering emotional support. The experience of caring about other individuals can be the foundation for young children to become prosocial. "Within a friendship, children can develop altruistic values, that is, prosocial behavior motivated by concern for others rather than the expectation of personal reward" (Riley et al., 2008, pp. 45–46). Infant–toddler peers look to each

36   Distinctive Infant–Toddler Social Encounters in Childcare

other for joint play experiences, appreciate and learn from each other's perspectives, and may find security and comfort in being with peers at stressful times (Recchia & Dvorakova, 2012). In this sense, friends can be a powerful resource for emotional comfort, soothing, and security.

FRIENDSHIP EXPERIENCES AND SOCIOCULTURAL CONTEXT

Babies go through significant developmental changes in the first few years of life. The individual infant's age and newly developed capabilities and skills will contribute to the relationship-building process (Degotardi & Pearson, 2014). For example, infants are becoming more proficient in their motor skills and acquiring one of the most salient developmental milestones in life: independent walking. This newly acquired mobility enables infants to become more independent and competent.

Let's recall the story of Clara, 12 months, and Luke, 11 months, featured in the previous section. When Clara was pre-mobile, most of her interactions took place one on one and focused on Luke predominantly. As previously explained, Clara and Luke exhibit mutual preference. Once mobile, infants start seeking proximity toward a specific social partner (Miller, 2000). For instance, Clara started walking independently around her first birthday. With her newly acquired developmental milestone, she could explore her surroundings willingly. Thus, the nature of social interactions can be transformed, resulting in more reciprocal exchanges among social partners (Raikes & Edwards, 2009). Consequently, the dynamic of social interactions with caregivers and peers changes. Clara, for example, began to initiate more interactions with peers, especially two older peers. The frequency of peer interaction among Clara, Amelia, and Emma increased.

> *Sarah (caregiver) gets a towel and gives it to Emma, 16 months, when Emma runs to the shelves and points to a blue bubble container, repeating "Buba." Amelia, 17 months, helps to get the towels and puts them on the floor. Clara, 13 months, walks around them with a smile on her face. Clara, Amelia, and Emma chase the bubbles as Sarah blows them.*

Infants and toddlers have their own personal characteristics, preferences, temperaments, and unique needs, all of which influence individual differences in infant–toddler peer relationships. The connection between developmental change and relationship development with caregivers and peers, particularly in times of a significant developmental transition, should be noted (Shin & Lee, 2011). Social partner preference and relationships evolve along with developmental changes (Howes et al., 1994; Lee, 2006; Raikes & Edwards, 2009; Rochat, 2001; Shin & Lee, 2011). Infant–toddler

Friendships Among Infant-Toddler Peers   37

caregivers must keep this in mind as they nurture and support the development of friendships among infant and toddler peers.

Role of Conflict in Building Relationships

Young friends prefer to be with each other as they engage in social play. Yet, they can also get into periods of discord. Peer conflict is an opposition between two children (Hartup et al., 1988; Hay, 1984). Conflict should be distinguished from aggression or antisocial behavior. Unlike aggression, conflicts are about disagreements and occur for numerous reasons: disagreements about possession of objects or the play environment; disputes about play ideas; curiosity and exploration; and dominance over one's peers (Caplan et al., 1991; Chen et al., 2001; Hay & Ross, 1982; Licht et al., 2008). Conflict can be frequent and common in early childhood environments. Most common peer conflicts among infants and toddlers involve object-possession struggles (Ashby & Neilsen-Hewett, 2012; Brenner & Mueller, 1982; Caplan et al., 1991; Chen et al., 2001; Eckerman & Peterman, 2001; Hay & Ross, 1982).

Researchers offer varied interpretations of children's object-oriented conflicts and social capabilities. For instance, Brownell and Brown (1992) claimed that struggle over toys appears to be more about the children not knowing how to play together than actual aggression. Curiosity and the drive to explore seemed to be the primary motivations leading children into conflicts in their second year of life (Licht et al., 2008). Conflict can offer valuable opportunities to further develop social understanding.

As seen in the anecdote below, Emily and Anna exhibited physical struggles and conflicts around the possession of objects.

> *Anna, 11 months, plays with the wagon. When Emily, 15 months, comes near, Anna looks at Emily, trying to go into the wagon by putting her leg inside. Emily tries to push Anna's hands and body while Anna shakes the wagon using both hands. Emily stops pushing, looks at Anna, and then walks away.*

Clearly, a conflict occurred between Emily and Anna. The interaction ended abruptly. We may want to pause here and wonder about infants' true intentions behind those actions. Emily clearly showed her intention of possessing the object, the wagon. She pushed Anna away to claim her ownership of the wagon. But what might be Anna's intention? When Anna realized that Emily was approaching the wagon, she tried to go into the wagon. Was this Anna's way of claiming ownership of the wagon? Was Anna physically shaking the wagon to show her interest in the wagon? What did Anna really want to do with the wagon, or with Emily?

A few months later, Emily and Anna had another object-centered conflict around the wagon. The vignette below raises the possibility that the

38 Distinctive Infant–Toddler Social Encounters in Childcare

unsuccessful interaction might have resulted from the miscommunication between these two infants rather than the exerted force or physical struggle.

> *Anna walks over to the wagon, goes in, and stands up, holding the handle of the wagon. Emily walks over, grabs the handle with Anna, and says, "Hi." Anna vocalizes "ah-ah," smiling at Emily. Anna then sits in the wagon and looks at Emily. Then Emily starts pushing the wagon for Anna.*

We can suppose that Anna's true intention was to gain attention from her friend, Emily, and play together. That might be why she tried to go into the wagon in the first anecdote. Her intention was not read by Emily correctly at first. But later, the conflict episode offered these friends the chance to compromise and better see each other's viewpoints. Eventually, Anna finally got pushed by Emily in the wagon. These two infants could participate in coordinated joint play when they interpreted each other's intentions. These anecdotes underscore that object-related conflicts may ultimately be beneficial to achieving social reciprocity.

Friends can indeed engage in conflicts. How about the conflict that arises between caregivers and infant–toddler friends?

> *Ryan, 26 months, is a very energetic, playful child. Ryan climbs on a small group table. He then looks around to see if someone is watching. When Rosa (caregiver) says, "Feet on the ground, please. We don't go up on the table," he smiles at Rosa widely. Ryan then laughs loudly, "A-ha-ha-ha." Calvin, 27 months, Ryan's friend, is on the floor, looking at Ryan smiling. Calvin follows what Ryan is doing, laughing loudly, "A-ha-ha-ha." Ryan climbs down from the table. Both Ryan and Calvin then pull every book from the bookshelf and leave them in a pile on the floor. When Ryan steps up and stomps on the big book, Calvin follows Ryan. The page of the book is torn apart. When Rosa asks them to put the books away, they pretend they cannot hear Rosa, giggling.*

Friends are excited to see each other. They have an enthusiastic way of engaging with each other. Sometimes, their energy might give them the courage to try more outrageous behavior together, inadvertently resulting in minor destruction. In addition, being friends allows Ryan and Calvin to step out of the boundaries set by the caregivers. They intentionally break the classroom rules. This friend duo pushes the limits to see what they can get away with. Their behaviors can present challenges to infant–toddler teachers and provoke the caregiver's discomfort, or even frustration. Will you let two toddler friends continue their play to enjoy and develop their friendship? How will you find a balance between supporting infant–toddler friendships and promoting a sense of classroom community? The answer will not be simple. There is a great need to acknowledge the dilemma that caregivers may face in their daily practices and provide opportunities for caregivers to reflect and collectively strategize around the topic. As you read further in this book, you will find more discussion about the importance of reflection and collaboration.

We argue that understanding conflicts among infants and toddlers as a sole motive to acquire objects can be a reductive and misleading interpretation of children's capabilities. Peer conflicts present meaningful learning opportunities for young children as they get to exercise and practice negotiation, compromise, and social problem-solving skills (Corsaro, 1985; Kemple, 1991). Through conflicts, young children develop social understanding by considering others' points of view and forming relationships (Shin, 2012). Close friends also find a way to solve conflicts and continue playing (Brownell & Kopp, 2007). Therefore, it is crucial to position conflicts as important learning events that can ultimately foster positive relationships among infants and toddlers.

INFANT-TODDLER CAREGIVING TO SUPPORT FRIENDSHIPS AND SOCIAL EXPERIENCES

Infants and toddlers are social beings, and early childhood teachers play a powerful role in contributing to infants' and toddlers' emotional well-being and social development. Caregivers should be multiplayers and "take on various roles, from active observer to play facilitator, depending on infants' developmental status as well as their interests and needs" (Recchia & Shin, 2012, p. 1560).

Careful observation is key to learning about young children's development and thus valuing and respecting their unique traits (Wittmer, 2012). The scenario below shows how a caregiver can clearly understand a child's nonverbal cues and interests based on careful observation and be ready to build on their play as needed. The caregiver, Elektra, allowed the two infants space to engage in exploration together without interfering:

Mary, 9 months, looks at a color paddle on the floor in front of Osman and crawls toward it. Osman, 6 months, picks it up first and taps a ring with it (left hand). Mary looks at what he is doing. Soon the two infants look at each other. Osman reaches his right hand to Mary's face but does not actually touch her. Then Osman taps the ring with the paddle again with his left hand, and Mary watches him for a long while. Mary moves a little closer to Osman, who continues to play with the paddle. When Osman transfers the paddle to his right hand, he drops it between Mary and himself. The two infants try quietly to pick it up for a while. Osman takes it. Elektra then slides another paddle near Mary. Mary gets it. Holding their paddles, Osman and Mary, sitting next to each other, play independently and look around the room.

40 Distinctive Infant–Toddler Social Encounters in Childcare

Another vital role of the teacher is to foster the social capabilities of infants and toddlers. Caregivers, thus, bring more significant support and make adaptations to facilitate babies' free exploration of the environment, speak for the children, and encourage peer engagement, as illustrated in the anecdote below:

> *Ruby, 15 months, is at the slide, and Lewis, 20 months, goes into the riser to hide. Victoria (caregiver) says, "Where did Lewis go?" Lewis crawls out of the riser, looking at Victoria. Victoria says, "Peek-a-boo." Ruby comes down the slide, lowers herself to see inside the riser, and finds Lewis. Ruby sits on the floor, bangs the floor with both hands, and makes noises that communicate her excitement. Ruby then stands up and walks a few steps away. Victoria says, "Ruby, are you going to hide for Lewis?" Ruby turns around toward Victoria, brings both hands toward her face to cover it, and then walks fast toward the hallway. Victoria says, "There goes Ruby. She's hiding, Lewis. Go look for Ruby. Go look for her. Go . . . say Peek-a-boo. I see you."*

That teachers play a critical role in developing young children's early peer relationships and competencies is a widely accepted idea (Howes & Ritchie, 2002). Teachers in tune with infants and toddlers can more likely read the child's cues accurately, respond meaningfully, and when appropriate, speak for the child. Infant–toddler teachers not only support social interactions but, most importantly, they engage in playful moments with infants and toddlers. As illustrated in the anecdote above, Victoria's physical proximity and engagement in infant–toddler interaction and dialogue are vital to extending social interactions with others (Davis & Degotardi, 2015; Recchia & Dvorakova, 2012; Redder & White, 2017; Wittmer, 2008). Victoria fully engaged in peer interactions between Ruby and Lewis. She also was an active partner in infant–peer dialogue rather than a mere observer (Redder & White, 2017). In these ways, Victoria was able to support the children's social development and friendship experiences.

What if Victoria did not add in the encouragement? Would Ruby and Lewis have had the same playful experience or opportunity to extend their peer interaction? Even sensitive, responsive teachers might not necessarily encourage positive peer-peer exchange as they engage in teacher–child play. How even a well-meaning caregiver might miss the cues and not provide enough support for peer interaction will be discussed next.

Missing Cues: Potentially Hindering Relationships

Thus far, we have emphasized that early childhood teachers need to be attuned to the needs of infants and toddlers, supporting peer relationships and actively engaging in infant–toddler interactions. However, knowing exactly when to intervene can be challenging for teachers (Goodfellow, 2014).

Teachers often appear to interrupt a naturally occurring opportunity for peer interaction or physically move infants and toddlers to minimize conflicts, enforcing rules for peer interaction (Williams et al., 2010). In addition, teachers might hinder the further development of infant–toddler interactions with a concern for their safety (Davis & Degotardi, 2015; McGaha et al., 2011; Redder & White, 2017).

Infants and toddlers are learning how to coordinate and control the movement of their bodies in space. They might be "too rough" or not "gentle" to each other. Teachers can often be anxious and hesitant about infants' physical interactions with their peers because of the uncertainty concerning their safety (McGaha et al., 2011). When physical touch is involved, teachers may feel the tension between wanting infants to engage with their peers and not wanting them to engage (Redder & White, 2017). As illustrated in the vignette below, possible peer interaction was halted when teachers misread a child's cues, adhering strictly to classroom rules.

> *Jennifer, 16 months, is playing at the sand table. Jennifer walks over to Amanda, 15 months, with a cup filled with sand, drops the cup on the way, and spills the sand on the floor. Ann (caregiver) helps Jennifer put the sand back into the sand table, mentioning that sand stays in the sand table. Jennifer puts down the cup, walks to Amanda, and says "sand." Rebecca (caregiver), who is reading a book with Amanda, responds, "You can sit down and read with us." Jennifer looks at them and then walks back to the sand table, playing alone.*

As demonstrated in this anecdote, the caregivers did not clearly understand Jennifer's nonverbal and subtle communicative strategy. Bringing a cup of sand over to Amanda could signify a social invitation. Jennifer wanted to show the sand to Amanda and possibly wanted to play with Amanda at the sand table. When the classroom rule—"sand stays in the sand table"—was enforced, Jennifer walked over to Amanda and still made a social overture, saying "sand." Jennifer's social intention, however, was not comprehended by Rebecca, who was with Amanda. The caregiver, probably with good intentions, asked Jennifer to join her ongoing activity, reading with Amanda. Jennifer walked away from the scene and played at the sand table alone. The children's further development of possible social play was thus hindered. Seeing Jennifer's action only as a violation of the rules, as opposed to a communicative gesture, shortchanged a potential social engagement with Amanda. It is easy for a caregiver's premature intervention to cut short or limit infants' and toddlers' opportunities to further extend their social interactions.

We know that friendships happen with the youngest children. Infant–toddler friendships can be supported and deepened with the encouragement of teachers who believe in the comprehensive social competencies of infants and toddlers. Observant caregivers can help create opportunities for peer interaction, communicating with infants about their feelings and behaviors, thus promoting understanding and social scaffolding. This allows babies to exercise and refine their capabilities. It is also essential for teachers to carefully reflect on, reconsider, and overcome any misconceptions to fully acknowledge the prosocial capabilities of infants and toddlers in their classrooms.

DISCUSSION QUESTIONS

1. What role do friendships play in your life?
2. What are your thoughts about infant and toddler friendship? Can infants and toddlers have friends?
3. What learning opportunities do infant and toddler friendships present?
4. Thinking about your practice, how do you promote and nurture friendships among infants and toddlers?
5. How do you help infant and toddler friends negotiate conflicts?

CHAPTER 4

Creative Social Exchanges
Infant–Toddler Humor

Annie, 16 months, is sitting in a highchair while having her snack. She takes hold of her water cup and starts banging it on the table in front of her. The other infants—Nick, 13 months, and Julia, 14 months—sit around the table and listen to the sound, looking at Annie. Annie smiles and repeats the action, looking at her peers, who also have a big smile on their faces. Nick and Julia soon start to bang their own water cups on the table while looking at each other and laughing.

In this chapter we will look at creative social exchanges of infants and toddlers. The chapter will employ the existing humor literature to describe how infants and toddlers explore the world through their senses, bodies, and interacting with peers and adults, thus revealing their humorous frames of mind and actions. Humor will be defined as it is seen through the eyes and actions of infants and toddlers, and specific examples will be used to show how they produce and appreciate it, highlighting its sociocognitive developmental core.

When caregivers acknowledge the vitality of meaningful relationships, shared moments, and playful contexts, they share infants' and toddlers' humorous frames of mind and support the production of humor. With the use of several vignettes, we will illustrate how infants' and toddlers' humor is enacted in an infant room while highlighting the diversity of their abilities and needs. A classroom learning environment where infants and toddlers are given the time and space they need to playfully use materials and creatively engage in activities serves to support and scaffold humorous exchanges and respects infants' agency.

Last, we will show how infant–toddler humor can create a space of challenging interactions, either from the infant's/toddler's or the caregiver's perspective, while providing opportunities for learning and development.

HUMOR DEFINITION AND THEORIES

Infants and toddlers are social beings, and they enjoy interaction with others, both adults and peers. They have fun in exploring these interactions playfully and humorously. The introductory anecdote is an example of the social exchange among infants and how they produce and appreciate humor within social interaction. Smiling and/or laughing are the social indicators of humor and are apparent in the interactions of babies. Babies smile and laugh when they experience things that make them happy and that they consider fun. Within this framework of happiness and playfulness, many humorous experiences arise.

When talking about humor in babies, we need to refer to their abilities to appreciate and produce humor. Infants and toddlers appreciate humor by observing other infants and/or adults produce humor, thus recognizing the alterations in an event or action taking place and appreciating it as funny. They are aware of the norm, such as how something is used or how someone looks or acts. They have this information in their memory, and when they notice violations of this norm, they recognize the incongruity involved; once they resolve it, they consider the situation as funny. Experiences that violate their existing schemata can lead to laughter. The following vignette highlights a fun, playful, out-of-the-norm interaction.

> *The caregiver watches Katie, 22 months, who taps her belly. Then the caregiver taps Katie's belly and says "Knock knock, who's there?" Katie laughs out loud and begins to tap her belly saying "Knock knock, who's there?" repeating this several times.*

Also, infants and toddlers begin to produce humor when they themselves start to be playful and creative with what they know, or when they explore the limits of the adults around them, aiming to draw the attention of their peers and/or adults. Mireault and Reddy (2016) suggest that humor production "requires infants to be able to take an additional cognitive step . . . more active engagement with someone else's mind, their intention and expectations" (p. 16).

> *The toddlers are sitting in small groups having their breakfast. The caregiver gives a sandwich to each child and says whoever wants another one can ask. Liza, 34 months, finishes her sandwich and asks for a second one, and the teacher gives her one. Then when she is done with that one, she asks for another one. The caregiver says that there are other children who did not have their second one yet, so she cannot have a third one. Liza then jokingly says, "Then I will eat my finger." The caregiver smiles and replies, "No, you are not!" Liza laughs and says, "I will eat it, look at me" and pretends to be eating her finger while laughing. She then says, "OK, then I will eat my fruit!"*

Clearly, Liza has the cognitive capacity to play with ideas and with her caregiver's expectations.

Humor is a sociocognitive experience because it provides children opportunities to explore and exercise both their social and cognitive development (Loizou, 2005a). There is a need for an "audience"—a parent, a sibling, a caregiver, or a peer—for an experience to be considered humorous. The interpersonal and socioemotional aspects of the humorous experience, and the way others respond, highlight its success. Infants and toddlers engage in interactions with their caregivers in which they "co-construct intersubjectivity by imitating each other . . . creating rhythms and patterns of behavior and they make violations of these predictable patterns to maintain the excitement" (Singer, 2019, p. 32). Such interactive experiences result in social laughing, their first humorous reactions.

Akiko, 16 months, puts her yogurt on the table and uses both hands to tap it and splash. She looks at Flora and Nicky (caregivers) and laughs out loud. Then she stops and waits, looking at them. Flora and Nicky smile, and Nicky says, "That is silly but yogurt is for eating."

McGhee (1979), who has systematically explored children's humor development, categorized it in stages, with the first stage referring to Incongruous Actions toward Objects, beginning around the age of 2 years. This first stage refers to children's ability to interact with objects as they begin to display their pretend play skills, using these skills to purposefully override their existing knowledge/schemata of things and experiences. Typical humorous actions would be to use a toy banana as a telephone or to touch their nose and say "ear," while looking at an adult and expecting them to laugh as they would do themselves. Loizou (2004a), with her two theories of humor, Theory of the Absurd and the Empowerment Theory, extends McGhee's work and suggests that infants younger than 2 years produce and appreciate humor. For instance, they exhibit their cognitive abilities when involved in humorous events where they show how they can produce or appreciate incongruous events (e.g., place yogurt on their head and say "shampoo" or sit on a toilet with their diaper on and say "pee-pee"). Also, in violating their caregivers' expectations, they break the rules or do not follow their directions as a way to be humorous and empower themselves.

More specifically, Loizou (2005a) suggests that infants employ humor in the following ways. Through the Theory of the Absurd, infants are involved in incongruous actions, funny gestures, positions, sounds, and words, and incongruous use of materials.

Anthony, 21 months, puts a cone on his head and looks at his caregiver and laughs, saying "Hat." The caregiver laughs too, and that makes Anthony laugh harder, putting the cone on and off several times.

Within the Empowerment Theory, infants and toddlers produce and appreciate humor through purposeful or unintentional violation of someone's expectations. These theories and categories provide a framework that clearly describes infants' and toddlers' attempts to be humorous while providing a definition of humor as something out of the ordinary and viewing the whole experience as sociocognitive. These theories also highlight that as infants and toddlers are involved in humorous exchanges they exhibit and further develop both their social and cognitive skills.

It is quite evident that children's ability to play is related to their ability to appreciate and produce humor. Bergen (2019) points out the close theoretical partnership between play and humor and advocates the need for a play frame for humor to develop. She writes, "young children's humor attempts often are closely connected to their playful attitudes and behaviors and these early humor attempts usually serve to increase the playfulness of all participants" (p. 12). Loizou (2005b) confirms that infants are involved in play activity when producing humorous events. She highlights the connection between humor production and play by saying that infants play with materials, their bodies, and language while being humorous in the context of play—they basically translate play activity into humorous events. Moreover, in the same study, Loizou comments on how infants turn routines and rules that they are quite familiar with into play, thus acting "inappropriately" and violating their caregiver's expectations in order to be humorous.

Of course, laughter is one of the social indicators of humor. But infants and toddlers tend to laugh for various reasons, and not all of them can be categorized as humorous. Singer (2019) discusses sources of laughter that can be interconnected in a humorous event. These involve social laughing, where infants and toddlers exhibit their sense of agency; laughter from playing with ideas; incongruity-based humor; and pleasure to function, the pleasure they draw in mastering what they are participating in.

Types of Infant and Toddler Humor

Early on, young children show signs of producing and appreciating humor through smiles and laughter. Examples of these early humorous experiences include games such as tickling and peek-a-boo. The following vignette involves a peek-a-boo game begun by the caregiver that developed into a fun and humorous incident with Nicolas, who enjoyed the interaction through giggles and smiles.

> *Julia (caregiver) and Nicolas, 6 months, are sitting on the floor. Nicolas is in the bouncy seat and kicks his feet and hands while Julia is talking to him, making various sounds. Julia picks up a scarf and puts it in front of her face and waits for Nicolas to notice. She suddenly removes the scarf and says "peek-a-boo," looking him straight in the face. Nicolas smiles, giggles, and kicks his feet*

Creative Social Exchanges: Infant–Toddler Humor   47

while trying to reach for the scarf. Then Julia uses the scarf to put it in front of Nicolas's face and removes it quickly, saying "peek-a-boo" while smiling, and Nicolas responds in the same way, smiling and kicking his feet.

This vignette illustrates an interpersonal experience in which Nicolas begins to develop an understanding of himself and enhances his socioemotional well-being.

Silly sounds and voices, along with silly faces and actions, are common behaviors that infants and toddlers exhibit in their interactions with familiar adults and peers (Reddy, 2001). Infants who interact more with their caregivers tend to have more social humorous exchanges with adults rather than with their same-age peers. Often, communication elicited by adults as a means to develop a relationship with the infant can lead to humorous events. And once these are registered as a distinct schema for the infant, one that brings joy, fun, and positive interaction, they are repeated, and infants begin to initiate them. For instance, in the peek-a-boo vignette above, once Nicolas enjoys the experience a couple of times, he will initiate the experience with his caregiver, seeking attention, fun, and communication.

As described earlier, once infants have created an understanding of how things work, they act in ways that violate expectations, intentionally producing incongruous actions to elicit laughter.

Katie, 22 months, runs to the bathroom. She sits on the toilet with her clothes on. The caregiver follows her, sees her sitting on the toilet, and smiles. Katie looks at the caregiver and says "pee-pee"; she then laughs, and runs out of the bathroom.

This example suggests that Katie is aware that she cannot make "pee-pee" with her clothes on while sitting on the toilet, which makes her action funny.

Often, teasing is used to describe how young children are involved in humorous events. It is described as the way infants and toddlers act intentionally in violating the expectations of adults or in not complying with the rules set by adults (Reddy, 2001). The following scenario is an example of offering and withdrawing as a means to create a humorous interaction with the caregiver.

Andy, 11 months, is sitting in a highchair having his snack. The caregiver, Leisha, is sitting next to him, commenting on his food. She says how hungry she is and that she would like a bite of his banana. Andy looks at Leisha and extends his hand, holding a piece of his banana in front of Leisha's mouth. When Leisha moves closer and opens her mouth, Andy pulls his hand away and places the banana piece in his mouth, laughing. Leisha looks at him smiling and says, "You cheeky boy!" Andy laughs even more, banging his feet on the chair. He then picks up another piece of banana and makes the same move, pretending to offer it to Leisha. Once Leisha smiles, Andy pulls his hand away and eats that piece as well, laughing and giggling.

Andy intentionally offers the caregiver a piece of banana, while smiling, and when he sees her positive response, he withdraws the banana piece, laughing. He intentionally violates her expectations and finds this action funny. As in other humorous events, these actions are repeated by the child, who enjoys the situation every time, with increased laughing and chuckling. Apparently, there is a true and authentic relationship between Andy and his caregiver as they seem to know each other and are aware of each other's expectations (Degotardi & Pearson, 2014), which allows them to enjoy the humor in their interaction.

As infants and toddlers develop their movement skills, they are more able to participate in funny bodily actions, chasing each other or running away from adults. As they develop their play style though physical actions and interactions (Løkken, 2009), they use these behaviors to empower themselves, drawing joy in acting humorously.

Anthony, 19 months, tries to run off in the hallway area and Emily (caregiver) calls his name, telling him he needs to stay in the hallway space. Anthony laughs out loud, running off. Emily runs after him and helps him come back by giving him a hug and a smile, saying "Tricky boy." Anthony laughs again, repeating "Tricky boy."

Calvin, 21 months, goes behind the door of the dance space. The caregiver tells him that that's not a place to play. She calls his name, and he peeks behind the door, smiling at her, and then goes back again. He repeats this twice and then comes out.

These two vignettes suggest that infants and toddlers listen to their caregiver's directions, understand what the expectations are, and choose to ignore them; they thus intentionally violate directions, producing a humorous event, making them laugh. In her Empowerment Theory, Loizou (2004a) states that when infants and toddlers violate their caregivers' expectations, they are empowered and feel superior. Similarly, Reddy (2019) comments on how infants and toddlers experience agency when disobeying their caregivers.

"Clowning" is another term used to describe young children's humor production and refers to the actions they intentionally repeat to provoke laughter from others. In her work, Reddy (2001) claims that "infant clowns" tend to act in many ways, as described above, such as making funny faces, sounds, body movements, and absurd actions, violating expectations and rules or showing hidden body parts. All these behaviors that infants and toddlers exhibit when involved in humor are typical actions that adult clowns also employ (Reddy, 2001).

Additionally, linguistic production and appreciation of humor is evident when language development advances. The creation of funny words, the mispronunciation of words, and the mislabeling of things are all part of infants' humor repertoire. As they grow older, they play with words and taboo themes such as poo and pee. Play is the context during which children explore their environment and develop their relationships. During such play moments, infants and toddlers express themselves in different ways, use and misuse language, and watch the reaction of adults and peers to their actions. These reactions signal the appreciation of their actions as humorous.

Deron, 18 months, is sitting next to Annie (caregiver); they are reading books. Deron picks up a book with fruit pictures and begins to look at the pictures. Annie asks him to point to different fruits, and he purposefully begins to make mistakes. Annie says, "Point to the cherries," and Deron points to the grapes. Annie says "You, silly boy, those are the grapes!" Deron looks at her and smiles. Then Annie asks him to point to the banana, and he points to the apple, smiling and waiting for her reaction. Annie says, "You, silly boy—that is the apple." Deron enjoys this interaction, smiles, and looks at Annie with a cheeky expression.

In this scenario, Deron produces humor by purposefully pointing to the wrong picture of the fruits his caregiver is naming. Pleased with the reaction he gets, he repeats the humorous incident. His caregiver joins in his funny game and calls him "silly boy," acknowledging his attempt to be funny.

Sometimes, infants and toddlers experience humorous events in their environment, such as someone—a parent or sibling—telling jokes. An infant with an older sibling who enjoyed sharing jokes learned a joke of her own, and shared it with her caregivers. The joke was as follows:

Katie: Knock knock.
Caregiver: Who's there?
Katie: Boo!
Caregiver: Boo who?
Katie: Don't cry, I love you!

Katie, 22 months, was not completely aware of the double meaning of her joke, but she knew there was a relationship between the concepts of "joke" and "funny" and knew it would bring laughter. There are thus instances where infants say something and call it a joke, or they call themselves funny because they understand the linguistic elements of a joking situation. Hoicka and Akhtar (2012) suggest that from their second year children can create their own jokes and comprehend what makes them funny. It is generally believed that the use of humor, or joking, is a means of coping with situations or dealing with negative experiences because it allows opportunities to express suppressed negative feelings (McGhee, 2010).

PEER SOCIAL ENCOUNTERS AS A CATALYST FOR HUMOR DEVELOPMENT

Infants and toddlers who share the same space, time, toys, and adult caregivers develop a sense of belonging, a peer culture. This peer culture involves interacting with one another, sharing mutual interests and activities (Degotardi & Pearson, 2014), while negotiating, and co-constructing experiences that potentially lead to learning and development. Just as infants and toddlers understand when their peers are in distress through their facial expressions, in the same manner they can acknowledge the joy they feel in playful, creative acts, and thus in the humor events they produce. Their response to this is to share this joy through smiles and laughter and at times to copy their actions. As children's social skills develop and as they move from parallel play to more interactive play exchanges, they begin to share with their peers their humorous events. Thus, we commonly see infants and toddlers who are in group care copy each other, producing together a humorous event, or appreciating each other's attempts to create humor.

> *James, 16 months, runs toward the door making giggling noises. He turns his body around and sits on the floor while touching the door with his back. Andrew, 14 months, follows James and sits on the floor right next to him. James looks at Andrew and smiles. James begins to move his legs up and down, making even louder sounds, and turns to look at Andrew. Andrew laughs and copies his movements, moving his legs up and down. James repeats this action for a moment but then gets up, waits, and looks at Andrew. He then runs to another area of the room laughing. Andrew gets up as well and runs after James laughing.*

This scenario shows how infants create games together and copy each other, enjoying the process as a playful and humorous one. They find interest in each other's actions and copy them in order to enjoy the event and the interchange. There are other instances during which children's interactions can accidentally lead to an incongruent experience, and this immediately turns into a humorous game that they repeat and enjoy. For example, two children may be running on the playground and trip over each other without getting hurt, which then becomes a repeated playful and humorous exchange (Singer, 2019).

Infant–toddler interaction in group care provides multiple opportunities for social encounters, expression of one's own ideas, and understanding of how others communicate. All these opportunities help children begin to share the same intentions and goals, especially when the interaction is playfully creative and fun, as in the vignette below.

Creative Social Exchanges: Infant–Toddler Humor 51

> *Katie (22 months), Trevor (19 months), Adonis (18 months), and Akiko (15 months) are at the table having a snack, and Vicky (caregiver) is sitting with them. Vicky comments on Trevor's actions: "You are eating your delicious pretzels—yummy!" Trevor looks at her, smiling and shaking his body. Katie looks at him, smiles, and starts shaking her body too. Then she stops and says, "Shiaaakka," looks at Vicky, and laughs. Katie repeats the word, smiling and looking at the caregiver. Vicky lifts her shoulders up and with a puzzled smiley face says, "What was that, Katie?" In the meantime, Trevor repeats the word, smiling. Katie keeps repeating the word too, laughing. Akiko starts laughing while eating her snack and looking at Trevor and Katie. Then Trevor laughs out loud too, and Akiko and Katie along with Vicky start laughing out loud. Katie repeats the word, and Vicky asks again "What is that word 'Shiakka'?" Katie repeats the word, laughing.*

This anecdote suggests that infants and toddlers tend to create humor during different contexts of the day. During their eating routine, which involves them being in a group and sharing the same space at the table, they find opportunities to interact with one another, expressing and/or appreciating each other's humor while also copying each other's actions, as in the scenario above. These experiences of togetherness and belonging (Van Oers & Hännikäinen, 2001) clearly motivate infants and toddlers to act humorously, and as Engdahl (2011) contends, laughter appreciation is key to toddler play interaction.

"Infants and toddlers draw on one another's reactions as a form of emotional reassurance . . . with immediate feedback about which behaviors are regarded as acceptable and unacceptable by other members of the group" (Degotardi & Pearson, 2014, p. 94). Humorous events are an example of behaviors in which infants and toddlers seek their peers' reaction. After seeing and hearing smiles or laughter, they repeat the action, reinforced by the feedback they have received.

> *Alison, 18 months, is at a table having her snack. She looks at Katie, 22 months, who is on the floor going around and around, getting dizzy, falling down, and then getting up again. Each time she gets up, she looks at Alison. Alison watches her, laughs, and looks at her caregiver, saying "Katie funny!"*

Alison reinforces Katie's action, and Katie enjoys the positive feedback; in response to the smiles and being called funny, she repeats her humorous behavior.

Infants and toddlers who meet daily in the same context begin to develop a culture of togetherness, sharing the same goals and intentions. To be humorous, they creatively exploit the frame of play they encounter during their day-to-day interactions, routines, and activities.

CLASSROOM LEARNING ENVIRONMENTS AND CAREGIVER ROLES SUPPORT HUMOR

In considering the classroom learning environment, we need to unfold the contexts within which infants and toddlers have their day-to-day experiences in childcare. Feelings of safety and consistency are important in helping infants and toddlers experience humorous events, both in appreciating and producing humor. Reddy (2001) comments on the importance of "ensuring an emotionally safe or socially familiar context within which the individual can perceive the incongruity" (p. 248). When infants and toddlers are aware of their daily schedule and they have a sense of ownership of their space and toys, they have multiple opportunities to distort those experiences and objects to play strange stunts, thus acting humorously.

> *Keisha 19 months, is playing on the floor by the pretend play house area. She takes the pretend dishes and cups from the small table and places them in the pretend play sink. She then takes the sink—white rectangular container—out of the cupboard, empties all the dishes and cups on the floor, and sits in it. She looks at the caregiver, Elena, and smiles. Elena comments, "Are you in a boat?"*

The context of play and routines provide multiple opportunities for infants and toddlers to explore their interests and abilities in producing and appreciating humor, as seen in the scenario above where Keisha turns the use of play materials into a humorous event. It is also evident that Keisha and Elena have a trusting, meaningful relationship. Elena appears to be in tune with Keisha and her actions, thus allowing her to be playful and funny.

In order for humor to unfold in the day-to-day experiences of infants and toddlers, the role of the caregiver is crucial. Loizou (2004b) writes, "Caregivers, by providing quality care, being respectful, responsive, accepting, and open, create an environment that helps enhance children's humor" (p. 18). With these attitudes, caregivers induce a space for both creativity and playfulness, which are equally important for humor to unfold.

When caregivers are playful, flexible, and creative themselves, they are able to acknowledge infants' and toddlers' attempts to be humorous. But also, they can themselves be sources of humor. The following vignette points out the importance of caregivers' attitudes.

> *Nicolas, 18 months, is at the table having a snack. He looks at the other children on the floor. He puts his bowl on top of his container, looks at it, and says to Elena (caregiver), "funny," smiling and pointing at the bowl. Elena smiles back and comments, "So you think you are a funny boy!"*

It is evident that Nicolas's caregivers were playful and appreciated his humor, enjoying his humorous action. Their affective response was important for him to understand that he is appreciated and successful in producing a funny incident. Loizou (2004a) proposes that caregivers can encourage humor development by "being alert to children's actions and using the clues that children offer to teach and guide them to further children's social and cognitive development" (p. 20).

Furthermore, it is important for caregivers to observe children and provide them with enough time and space to explore their environment, to develop relationships with peers and adults, to test their abilities, and to use materials in creative ways, thus engaging in humorous behaviors without caregivers intervening. When provided enough time and space, children can begin to test the limits and find creative and humorous ways to exhibit what they know. As noted earlier, the production of humor involves knowing when something is incongruous, when something is out of the ordinary. When children develop enough schemata about concepts, relationships, and how a caring community works, they begin to purposefully violate these schemata to become humorous.

The caregivers can give infants and toddlers the opportunity to interact with their peers and also allow them to be independent and explore their environment and test their skills. For example, a caregiver can sit back and watch toddlers bang their cups on the table. Or, as the example below suggests, they can appreciate children's attempts at humorous behaviors through smiling or laughing.

> *Abigail, 15 months, sits at the table with Vanessa (caregiver) and draws with crayons. Abigail makes various facial expressions: furrowing her eyebrows, blinking her eyes, smiling, all while looking at Vanessa, who laughs at Abigail's expressions. Abigail repeats them and laughs out loud as well.*

A positive response (i.e., laughing at children's attempt to be humorous) sends the message that their attempt is understood and appreciated, providing infants the space to explore their abilities to produce humor and deepen their relationship with their caregivers.

Caregivers who appreciate children's freedom to explore and unfold their abilities tend to actively participate in their humorous events and comment on the children's actions. They find opportunities to use language and describe their actions and behavior, but they also take part in the event through smiles or laughter. Hoicka and Gattis (2012) refer to parental clowning and how parents, by laughing while acting silly, support infants in considering the experience a positive one. It is important that when infants and toddlers invite caregivers to join in an activity, they do so by acknowledging their humorous behaviors. For example, teachers can peek back at the children between their legs to say hello or repeat their funny gestures or facial expressions.

> *Abigail, 15 months, puts her head in Valerie's (caregiver) lap and lifts up her bottom. Valerie smiles and extends her hand, waving and saying hello to Abigail from between her legs. Abigail gets up and looks at Valerie, smiling. Valerie smiles back, and Abigail repeats. Valerie extends her hand and waves, saying hello and smiling. Abigail lifts her head up and looks at Valerie, smiling too. Abigail repeats this action four times, and Valerie follows up on it, smiling with Abigail.*

The activity here is initiated by Abigail, and her caregiver, Valerie, follows her lead. Accepting offers from children is one of the many roles caregivers play. They can respond to children's invitations to play and at times copy children's behaviors, following their lead. Thus, caregivers can pretend along with children to drink tea or to hold a baby or to talk on a phone. The caregiver engages with the children, actively participating in children's activities, becoming part of their scenario, and adding to it. By acting in this way, they show how such behaviors are acceptable and valued (Bergen, 2019).

Another important aspect of the caregiver's role is the constant commenting and communication that takes place between caregivers and children. Loizou (2004a) believes that caregivers should "provide linguistic and social scaffolding for infants who need assistance in acquiring the necessary tools to socialize, so they can enjoy humor as a group" (p. 20).

Sometimes, however, infants and toddlers use humor that their peers do not appreciate. Such cases include infants and toddlers taking each other's food or throwing down their water cups or even taking their toys while laughing and maybe running away. In addition, there are cases during which children do not understand the humor created by peers or caregivers, perhaps due to their difficulty in symbolic representation or their inability to take another person's view (Bergen, 2019). In such cases, caregivers must provide space for infants and toddlers to express their humor while at the same time protect others who do not understand or feel uncomfortable with it. It is thus important to intervene and play liaison in order to protect children who do not enjoy the specific humor. As described in the following vignette, the caregiver is present to acknowledge attempts of humor and at the same time to explain how others are feeling about the humorous behaviors taking place.

> *Drayvon, 22 months, runs over to Julie, 24 months, and pulls her hat. He puts it on his head and runs around the classroom laughing. Julie looks at him and whines, saying "my hat!" The caregiver observing this event comments, "Drayvon, I know you are trying to be funny, but Julie does not like you taking her hat right now."*

Humor is an individual and cultural act where engagement takes many forms. Reddy (2019) writes, "Cultures not only differ in the content of their jokes, but also in their styles of humor" (p. 193). There are instances when adults, caregivers, and/or parents attempt to make babies laugh, or they tend to tease them. This is what Reddy refers to as "family specific humor," times during which children and adults share and enjoy moments of cultural interaction. All families share their own jokes and ways of teasing each other. Examples include a mom who tickles her baby right after bath time, a toddler who hides behind the bathroom door when her mom calls for a bath, a sibling who makes silly moves and noises with her body to make her baby brother laugh, a dad who calls his toddler "silly goose," making goose sounds every time the child runs away at diaper-change time. Teasing is one way that infants and toddlers, as well as adults, might re-create culture as they play with cultural norms in an effort to make culture a live process (Reddy, 2019).

Curriculum: Materials/Toys and Playful Activities as Important Elements for Humor

Any childcare setting that follows an appropriate curriculum includes a variety of objects and toys that relate to infants' and toddlers' play needs (e.g., riser boxes, small chairs, slide, ramp, hats, scarves, teapots, cups, tape, baby dolls); physical needs such as eating, sleeping, and changing; and materials needed in day-to-day activities (e.g., sponges, bibs, food, bins, smocks, bowls, shoes, pants). Infants and toddlers become quite familiar with these objects/toys and their use, so that in a playful and humorous mood they may misuse them as a way to exert power. The following scenario is characteristic of this.

> *Nicolas, 20 months, is at the table. Elia (caregiver) gives him a sponge and asks him to clean up his space. Nicolas puts the sponge on his head, stops, and looks at Elia, smiling. Elia looks at him and smiles back. She gets the sponge and asks him if he thinks the sponge is a hat. Nicolas says "yeah" and giggles. When Elia asks Nicolas if he thinks he is a funny boy, he says "yeah!," laughing.*

Nicolas is quite familiar with the process of cleaning up the space where he eats, so he takes advantage of this knowledge to change his actions, exerting power over the material, the situation, and his caregiver. He expects his caregiver to react to his inappropriate behavior, but he is not afraid to engage in it, expecting a gentle response.

Infants and toddlers are engaged mostly in free play; they engage in pretend play, play hide and seek, chase each other, read books, play with bubbles, jump on a trampoline, play with scarves, puzzles, blocks, and so much more. When they are free to choose what to play with, and where and how to play, they are given opportunities to be creative and playful. This provides the perfect setting for humorous behaviors.

56   Distinctive Infant–Toddler Social Encounters in Childcare

Andy, 19 months, puts the block container on his head. He walks around, bumping and raising the container up, smiling. Vanessa (caregiver) looks at Andy, laughing. She says, "Andy, you can't see with that on your head." Andy walks some more, bumps somewhere, and you can hear him laugh until he decides to take it off.

Pretend play is one of the activities during which infants and toddlers can show their creativity, as they use both acquired and new concepts to build on their experiences and to create and appreciate humorous events.

Akiko, 15 months, grabs a block and pretends to eat it. Mary (caregiver) sits down close to her, grabs a block, and pretends to eat it too. Akiko says, "Hot, hot, hot" moving back, bouncing her feet and flapping her hands. Mary pretends the block is hot and puts it on the floor, saying "Ouch ouch!" She looks at Akiko and laughs.

> *The caregiver takes baby Larry, 6 months, out of his air chair when his father enters the room. Katie, 21 months, sits in Larry's chair, holding a baby doll and a baby bottle, and bounces, laughing out loud, looking at Larry's father, who touches her gently and says, "You, silly goose." Katie feeds the baby doll while in the air chair and then tries to buckle herself in. She then gets out, gets the baby doll, and takes her to a highchair by the table and buckles her in.*

Akiko and Katie exhibit pretend play behaviors and acknowledge the potential humor in the situation. They both enjoy these behaviors as a joking experience due to the cues of the adults, the caregiver, and Larry's father, respectively. Hoicka and Martin (2016) suggest that 2-year-olds distinguish between pretending and joking, and that they are capable of understanding the intention behind an act they observe. They also comment that the intentional cues in an action (e.g., laughter or use of words such as "silly goose") are important for toddlers to distinguish a joke.

Humorless Environments That Restrain Humor Experiences

An environment that is strictly based on rules and firmly follows the same routines for all infants and toddlers—such as the same time for eating, diaper changing, sleeping, and structured play activities—with little or no flexibility, is one that provides limited space for humorous behaviors to be acknowledged, valued, or encouraged.

The 2-year-old group has just had their breakfast in the kitchen area, which is across the hall, next to the principal's office. The caregiver asks them to hold hands with a friend to walk back to their classroom. On the way to the classroom, Gorki, 28 months, and Stephan, 26 months, look at each other smiling and then run to the small slide on the side of the hall area and begin to climb. They giggle and turn to look at their caregiver. The caregiver, in a stern voice, states that it is time to return to the classroom and that they are not allowed to play in that area. Gorki and Stephan go back walking backward. The caregiver moves close to them, holds their hands, and says, "You need to be good boys and follow the rules. Walk properly."

Nicky, 30 months, and Julia, 26 months, are sitting at a high table in their classroom having their lunch. Nicky picks up her cup, drinks some water, and then begins to shake it while smiling and looking at Julia. Water comes out of the cup onto the table, and she says "Rain!" Julia watches her and smiles. She picks up her own cup and shakes it as well, letting water come out on the floor. They both look at each other, laughing and jointly say "Rain!" The caregiver notices their action and picks up both of their cups and says, "You should not play with your water!"

Potential humor events, like the ones described above, involve challenging interactions and experiences for infants/toddlers and caregivers; when they are not in sync about the funniness of the actions, it is hard for the events to be appreciated by both sides. Caregivers who view such humorous events only as a violation of rules will certainly control the children and negate their attempts. Lack of playfulness and flexibility, with an emphasis on control, does not allow caregivers to see the empowering aspects of humorous experiences. Clearly, this can have a negative effect on the relationships they develop with children (Reddy, 2019).

As a basis for infant and toddler learning and development, when meaningful relationships are not developed authentically, humorous interaction is bound to fail. Moreover, as caregivers are expected to role-model for infants and toddlers, when children aim to use humor, it is important that their caregivers refer to the interaction they are sharing as funny, humorous, or silly so that children begin to get a sense of the context of these humorous interchanges (McGhee, 2019). Also, when and if caregivers choose to use humor in their exchanges with infants and toddlers, they need to ensure that it involves concepts that infants and toddlers have already acquired. Distortions of concepts that children have not yet acquired (e.g., animals with wrong body parts; a cat with feathers) have no point and can lead children to misinterpretations and perhaps feelings of insecurity.

Caregivers can and should employ opportunities for humorous exchanges because they create a fun, emotionally safe, and creative environment for infants and toddlers to explore their surroundings, strengthen their interactions, learn about the world, develop, and enjoy themselves.

DISCUSSION QUESTIONS

1. What role does humor play in your life?
2. Do you take note of smiles and laughter in your group setting? When do they seem to happen most often?

3. What are the learning elements in producing and/or appreciating humor for infants and toddlers?
4. How do you feel about violating rules in your infant–toddler setting?
5. Thinking about your practice, do you provide enough opportunities for infants and toddlers to interact, become playful, and be creative?

Part II

CREATING INTERPERSONAL ENVIRONMENTS THAT SUPPORT RESPONSIVE CARE

CHAPTER 5

The Complex Role of Infant–Toddler Professionals

Care, Love, Diversity, and Identities

I can remember going into it just a month ago feeling overwhelmed with how little the infants seemed. Now, I realize that, yes, they are "babies," but they are also so intelligent, so explorative, and fascinated, and it's wonderful to see. I look forward to this week and seeing Clara! It's amazing how each week I look more and more forward to going in as my bond has become stronger with Clara, and with that the day can seem more meaningful and pleasurable, interacting and observing Clara's development. . . . Connecting with Clara and building a relationship with her was really special to me. I think in any classroom setting it is natural to become attached to the children you are surrounded by. That is for sure the most stimulating thing for me, and I know that is why I love being around children so much! The bond that one can form with a child, and even an infant as small as Clara, is really remarkable. Professionally it is something I never take for granted, and I cherish each and every bond I have with students . . . no matter what, children will connect with you if your passion and love for them is there as well. (Sarah, Infant Practicum Student)

This chapter considers the complex role that infant–toddler teachers play in young children's development and learning, navigating through an intricate web of emotions, feelings, and personal and professional experiences. Discourses of care, education, and love are deeply interwoven in infant–toddler professionals' everyday practices. While the field of early childhood education and care has come to acknowledge there should be no division between care and education, love tends to be invisible and silenced. We fully recognize that relationships involve interpersonal relatedness and emotional experience and discuss a critical need to reclaim love in the field of early childhood education and care. Next, the strong emotional connections that exist in daily practice also call for a need to scrutinize the social-emotional aspects of professionals' work and the emotional labor that professionals experience. Finally, we discuss the significance of validating and appreciating diverse infants' and teachers' lived experiences to become more authentic, thoughtful, and intentional professionals.

BRINGING CARE, EDUCATION, AND LOVE TOGETHER

Relationship-based practice is at the core of what we do as infant–toddler teachers. Relationships are the basis for learning and development for very young children; they foster trust, warmth, reciprocity, socialization, and a sense of belonging (Degotardi et al., 2017). The chapter-opening anecdote shows how a student-teacher developed a special bond with an infant, Clara. Sarah felt joy being with babies through a close relationship. She added that the connection with children would always be possible if her passion and love for them were there. Inevitably, strong emotional bonds and loving relationships emerge and exist in our daily practice. Love becomes deeply embedded in our work and is integral to our practice. Yet, many teachers and researchers do have concerns talking about love (Shin, 2021b). The topic of love has long been considered taboo in the field (Page, 2011). Why are care and love absent in our discussion?

Discourses of Care, Education, and Love

One possible explanation for this absence of care and love is the long-held misconception in our field that care and education are two separate things. Education has also been perceived as higher or superior to caring (Van Laere et al., 2012), while caring has frequently been undervalued. Historically, caring was viewed as an extension of mothering. Caring for young children has been regarded as a woman's job. Because caring was linked to instinctive, motherly, and innate qualities, early childhood professionals' work was viewed as unprofessional and ordinary, something that anyone can do without formal training (Ailwood, 2008; Aslanian, 2015; Dalli, 2008; Lally, 1995). This gendered view of caring is problematic and responsible for low pay and low status for women working with young children. To professionalize the field, detaching from motherhood and care discourses was deemed necessary (Ailwood, 2008; Aslanian, 2015).

Consequently, affective aspects of early years practices were diminished. As Dalli (2006) states, "as we have moved closer to the goal of a professionalized sector, we have become more and more articulate about all the knowledge and skills that we consider important in professional teacher, but less and less clear about how, or even whether, to integrate love and care in this new construction of profession" (p. 6). The discussion around love and care became silenced.

Also, care and love are often situated in the affective domain. They are understood in professional practice as primarily feeling, emotion, or

The Complex Role of Infant-Toddler Professionals   63

personal traits that professionals should possess (Cousins, 2017; Goldstein, 1998). A commonly held and naïve notion of caring is imaged as gentle smiles and warm hugs (Goldstein, 1998). This notion obscures the complex and challenging aspects of our work with young children (Rockel, 2009). Caring is not about warm, fuzzy feelings. Caring is not about simple custodial work, such as supervising children and keeping them safe and clean. When we care, we engage in complex intellectual and pedagogical work, observing, listening, being present, and following babies' lead. "Caring is not something you are, but rather something you engage in, something you do" (Goldstein, 1998, p. 246). Caring is "extraordinary" work (Shin, 2015) and should be understood as an intellectual and pedagogical act.

Now there is a much-needed paradigm shift recognizing that care and education are inseparable. Both care and education have been considered legitimate parts of the pedagogical approach to learning (Page, 2017). We support the notion that we simultaneously care for and educate babies in our practice. However, love remains ignored and overlooked despite this more holistic conceptualization of care and education. So, where is love?

The notion of love has frequently been hidden behind constructs. It is because love is hard to define and measure. Love is complex, elusive, and abstract. Also, love will look different in different settings. Thus, as Page (2014) argues, "for too long, the concept of love in education has been masked by other terms which are different to love though they are equally important" (p. 120). The terms include care, warmth, responsiveness, highly valued, respect, and attachment. However, these terms describing the characteristics or the manifestation of love in our work do not necessarily mean the same thing as love (Page, 2011).

Jisu reflected on the intimate nature of infant–toddler care, which she saw as unique and different from other relationships.

> I wonder if such intimacy is the nature of infant care because my relationship with Liam was or had to be intimate from the beginning. In fact, from the second time I saw Liam I was already putting my arms around his body, shushing by his ears, rubbing his back, and cleaning his naked body. Such intimacy would not happen between two adults from the second day. Nevertheless, in the infant classroom, this happens from the first day teachers meet the infants. This is not something to take for granted, but to really appreciate and enjoy! I am loving this intimate relationship I'm forming with Liam as well as with other children in the classroom. (Jisu, Infant Practicum Student)

How could you explain these intimate feelings that Jisu was experiencing in a professional setting? Is care or warmth sufficient to describe the emotion Jisu developed working with babies? Is it possible to care for young children without love? Whether practitioners and researchers decide to talk about or not to talk about love and emotions, we cannot deny that emotion

64 Creating Interpersonal Environments That Support Responsive Care

and affection are there in our daily practice. Our everyday work with babies encompasses love, care, intimacy, and education. It is time to enunciate love more openly and straightforwardly and call for "a future where love and care sit re-visioned as (legitimate) elements of our professional discourse" (Dalli, 2006, p. 20).

Reclaiming Love as an Essential Component in Caregiving

Love is essential for human beings. Young children need to feel loved and valued. Children do not thrive without receiving loving attention (Manning-Morton, 2006). Early childhood professionals feel love for children (Recchia et al., 2018). Parents want professionals to love their children (Page, 2011). In other words, "love for students is an underlying assumption of the practices of many, many early childhood teachers" (Goldstein, 1998, p. 7).

Jools Page proposed the concept of professional love to legitimize love that encompasses intimacy between early childhood teachers and young children. Professional love signals that the love we provide as a teacher is qualitatively and distinctly different from maternal love or the romantic notion of love. In professional loving, teachers are self-aware of their feelings and able to decenter to see the world from the view of young children (Page, 2014). The ability to decenter means that professionals forego their own opinion, imagine being in the child's position, and concentrate fully on the child's needs (Page, 2017). Teachers will thus respond sensitively to the needs of the children, be more attuned with them, and create emotional intimacy and reciprocal relationships.

Professional love, in this sense, connects to the ethics of care. Nel Noddings believes that engrossment and attention are central to ethics of care. First, the one-caring (or carer) needs to be attentive. The one-caring needs to hear and understand what the cared-for is feeling and trying to express. "Attentive love listens, it is moved, it responds, and it monitors its own action in light of the response of the cared for" (Noddings, 2002, pp. 136–137). The one-caring becomes more engrossed in the one being cared for, directing mental attention to and focus on the cared-for to gain a greater understanding. In a caring encounter, the cared-for recognizes the caring and responds back in certain ways. With reciprocity, teachers and babies can experience a deepened relationship and heightened level of emotional intimacy.

The scenario below shows how Rose and Becky experienced professional love and shared affectionate encounters.

Rose, 16 months, walks to Becky (infant teacher), touches Becky's shoulder, and puts her head on it. Becky smiles and turns her head to Rose and asks, "You wanna go to the dance space, Rose?" Rose giggles and steps up onto Becky's thigh. Becky hugs Rose tightly for a while. Then Rose walks to the shoe rack

The Complex Role of Infant–Toddler Professionals   65

and picks up her shoes. She puts them on the floor and fingers the shoelaces. Becky talks to Rose from a distance, "Rose . . . you still need a diaper change." Rose turns her head and looks at the inside of the room (toward Becky). Soon she returns to her shoe exploration, babbling "raruli . . . wee . . . wab . . ." Becky helps other children get ready first. When she puts a shoe on her left foot (about half), Rose looks up at Elektra (teacher) and smiles widely, sounding "Ah!" Elektra giggles. Rose continues to play with her shoe for quite a long while . . . Becky approaches her and suggests to her softly, "Rose, you need to change your diaper first, then you can put your shoes on." But Becky does not interfere or force Rose, who tries to put the shoe on by herself. Finally, Rose puts it on and tries to stand up. Becky responds with genuine enthusiasm, "You got it on! You put your shoe on! Hooray! You put it on!" Rose stands up and smiles brightly, looking at Becky.

This anecdote opened with such lovely, affectionate encounters between Rose and Becky. Without exchanging verbal interaction, they shared such intimate moments through touching, leaning toward, putting a head on the other's shoulder, and smiling. When Becky asked Rose if she wanted to go to the dance studio, Rose was quite excited. Becky's plan was to change everyone's diapers and get everyone ready for the dance studio. Rose took a while to put on her shoes by herself. However, Becky did not rush or force Rose to get a diaper change. Becky did not interrupt Rose's ongoing activity. Instead, Becky removed her needs from the equation and fully absorbed herself in Rose's needs. This professional love gave Rose the space and time to develop her self-help skills and feel pride and self-confidence in her ability to exercise them. "Babies and young children need to feel accepted, liked and loved if they are to feel comfortable about themselves and what they can do" (Page et al., 2013, p. 49). Clearly, Rose was supported, loved, and respected.

Love is highly apparent and deeply embedded in daily practice (Recchia et al., 2018). Reciprocal relationships can bring joy, emotional rewards, and love to teachers and babies. Many professionals may choose to use the alternative, perhaps partly synonymous, terms. Yet, these terms will not be able to capture the depth and intensity of feeling that love entails. Page (2018) refers to the "pseudonymization of love," which waters down the meaning and could restrict love in practice. Indeed, the work of infant and toddler teachers involves care, education, and love. "The affective won't go away. It's always there, whether researchers admit it or not. The plain old fact of the matter is that teachers and children have hearts, and those hearts play an enormous part in the teaching/learning process" (Foss, 1995, cited in Goldstein, 1998, p. 30).

Loving care is more than a set of teaching strategies; it is a way to nurture babies' emotional well-being through strong emotional connections. As Gopnik (2010) says, "it's not so much that we care for children because we love them, as that we love them because we care for them" (243). It is through the responsive caregiving process that professional love unfolds. When we admit that love is a core element of our professional identities, not in conflict with professionalism (Recchia et al., 2018), we can reclaim love as an essential component in infant–toddler caregiving.

CONTEMPLATING EMOTIONAL LABOR

Touch is an integral part of everyday interaction between infant–toddler teachers and babies. Although touch is an important way of demonstrating love to young children (Gerhardt, 2004; Murray, 2022), the subject of touching young children has become controversial. Physical touching and the hands-on aspect of caring are constructed as dangerous. Many teachers are concerned about child abuse or improper touch and are confused, fearful, anxious, and wary (Page, 2011; Piper & Smith, 2003). This sad, crisis-ridden situation can threaten our babies' development and well-being.

Ambivalent Feelings About Touch

Caring for babies is inherently intimate. We change diapers. We rock babies to sleep. We hold babies to feed a bottle. We need to lift babies up. We clean babies up after eating or messy play. We stroke and soothe crying babies. Suppose we worry about the possible misunderstanding of physical aspects of our work and thus shy away from being intimate during routine-based moments. In that case, we lose a crucial opportunity to connect with babies.

The reflection below illustrates the powerful emotional engagement and love that takes place between Lucinda and Maria during routine-based practice:

I really enjoy Maria's nap time; I consider this a very important time to bond with each other. First, when taking the bottle, Maria makes eye contact with me, touches my face, and I sometimes talk to her. Then, when it is time to sleep, she just puts her head on my chest and I sing to her when she cries a little bit because of the tiredness, and that calms her down. (Lucinda, Infant Practicum Student)

Lucinda and Maria demonstrated that touch is important in experiencing care, love, affection, emotional connection, and emotional security. Intimacy and strong emotional connections emerge through affective touch. Touch, therefore, is integral in our daily practice and critical in babies' development and well-being. Considering that "being lovingly held is the greatest spur to development" (Gerhardt, 2004, p. 40), we must ponder how to show love

The Complex Role of Infant–Toddler Professionals   67

appropriately and wholeheartedly through affective touch rather than fear and shy away from touch. Touch is a powerful nurturing force.

It is also important to acknowledge individuality. There might be infants and toddlers in your care who have sensory sensitivity. Some babies simply might not want to be cuddled or swaddled. Some might dislike touching certain textures. Some might not want to be touched. Reading, hearing, and listening to babies is essential to learning more about their specific needs, likes, and dislikes. Lara shared:

> As I begin spending more time with her, I will learn more about her individual routine, habits, her likes, and dislikes. For example, I have observed that she gets fussy and squirms during a diaper change. She turns away from me and becomes very distressed. She does not like to wear socks and shoes. So, it is a real challenge to get her diaper changed and get ready to go outside to the playground. However, I found that if I sing or hum to her or let her hold something, she is a lot calmer. I tried humming "Twinkle Little Star," and it was amazing to see how much calmer she became. (Lara, Infant Practicum Student)

Figuring out this baby's preferences enabled Lara to take care of her appropriately and provide more individualized and responsive care. As a result, Lara was more attuned and started developing and enjoying a strong bond with the baby. The sense of touch is one of the ways for babies to learn about themselves and the world around them. Babies do have preferences and sensory sensitivity; they can be over-sensitive or under-sensitive to touch or textures. Some babies love playing with sand and do not mind their sand-filled diapers, while another baby will not even touch the sand. Some might be easily annoyed by itchy, scratchy clothing tags. Some might avoid certain textures, like slimy or sticky things. Some love fingerpainting and, perhaps, do not mind painting their whole body. We need to really listen to babies, figure out their individual preferences and needs, and respect and be responsive to their ways of being while supporting them to explore different tactile and sensory experiences.

Emotionally Present and Charged

Thus far, we have discussed how our daily practices supporting infants and toddlers involve emotions, intense feelings, and complex, multifaceted relationships. To establish a positive relationship with babies, infant–toddler teachers invest enormous amounts of time and energy to read, hear, and understand babies in their caring encounters. This strong commitment to loving care can become a source of difficulty for teachers and place extra pressure on them, as it requires both an intellectual and an emotional commitment (Goldstein & Lake, 2000; Osgood, 2006).

Emotional labor is one aspect of infant–toddler caregiving that has received relatively little attention. The term "emotional labor" was coined by Arlie Hochschild (1983). Looking at service providers, specifically flight attendants, Hochschild studied how emotional labor impacted their well-being and job performance. Emotional labor refers to the process of managing feelings and expressions to create a publicly observable face and bodily display as part of one's work role. In the context of service work, a person is compelled to express socially desired emotions. This means the person often restricts or limits their authentic emotional displays to provide an expected high level of customer service. This emotional labor can result in negative outcomes for some workers, such as job stress and burnout (Purper et al., 2023).

Infant–toddler teachers engage in emotional labor and navigate many emotional demands. The way that teachers experience emotional labor is distinctively different from other professionals or service providers. Studies on emotional labor primarily focus on single-point interactions between service employees (i.e., flight attendants or nurses) and clients. On the other hand, teachers see the young children ("clients") in their care on a daily basis, having *prolonged* engagements within the context of relationships (Purper et al., 2023). Unlike flight attendants or other service providers, teachers also pay attention to young children's family backgrounds and provide care based on their accumulated knowledge of children. Our work involves connecting closely with children, families, and other professionals. Thus, due to the highly interpersonal nature of our work, we experience a wide range of emotions while working with infants and toddlers (Davis & Dunn, 2018).

Early childhood teachers are called upon to continuously engage in emotional labor during their working hours. Goldstein and Lake (2000) state, "at times even the most committed teacher's capacities for ongoing caregiving are exhausted due to the inherently unequal nature of a caring teacher-student relationship" (p. 862). Early childhood teachers are expected to remain positive, calm, and encouraging in interactions with parents, other teachers, and children (Purper et al., 2023). Teachers often push their own emotions aside to be sensitive to children's emotions. Negative feelings, such as stress, disgust, anger, sorrow, irritation, or being overwhelmed, are considered unprofessional and thus not allowed (Colley, 2006; Elfer, 2015; Elfer & Dearnley, 2007). Consequently, teachers "learn above all to control and manage their own feelings of disgust, anger, sorrow and fear . . . being kind and loving, warm and friendly, gentle and affectionate are . . . qualities of a caring person. Despite the fact that . . . they constitute an impossible ideal" (Colley, 2006, p. 17). But we are human. We might occasionally meet a child to whom we react negatively (Grossman, 2008). However, negative emotions have been considered unprofessional, especially regarding children. Many negative emotions have thus been hidden or masked to show professionalism (Page & Elfer, 2013).

Early childhood educators engage daily in physical, mental, and highly emotional work, as illustrated in one teacher's reflection below:

I feel like lately I've been pretty emotionally exhausted. During the morning drop-off time, Shanna, 17 months, has been clinging to her mom and crying. Mom has to hand crying Shanna over to me. Sometimes, mom is almost like prying Shanna off her leg and hands her over to me. And Shanna is like an alarm going off, crying and crying. I hold her and walk around to calm her down. As soon as I put her down though, she starts crying again. If I don't pick her up right away, she is crying intensely, almost like screaming and yelling. When she sees other babies crying, she will cry too. She needs to be, like, glued to me. At the end of each day, I feel like an alarm is going off in my brain. I can still hear her crying. It is exhausting. This week felt hard and long and I am emotionally off.

A crying baby can rattle infant–toddler teachers and parents because we tend to feel a sense of urgency when babies cry. It is perfectly natural for humans to experience various emotions. Teachers might sometimes feel out of control and find it difficult to regulate their feelings, which are all part of natural human emotions. Just as babies need support to develop emotional understanding, teachers need support to reflect on emotions, positive and negative, in early childhood settings. Open discussions among practitioners may help reflect on practices, emotions, and feelings. "If ignored or denied, such feelings have the potential to do harm. Like steam in a pipe, feelings unexpressed or ignored will escape somewhere and outburst toward an undeserving child" (Grossman, 2008, p. 147). The better we understand ourselves, the more likely we are to be able to validate young children's emotions instead of stifling them (Jacobson, 2018). Thus, creating institutional spaces (e.g., Work Discussion) for teachers to fully understand, reflect, and cope with their own feelings is critical (Elfer, 2012). Teachers' jobs often take a toll on their emotional, physical, and mental well-being, leading to teacher burnout and stress. Implementing a supportive, "safe space" environment is critical to avoiding emotional labor burnout. The need to establish support systems will be discussed in Chapter 6.

APPRECIATING DIVERSE LIVED EXPERIENCES

Infant–toddler teachers are commonly called on to nurture young children's and their families' cultural identities and practices. Teachers practice culturally responsive care by partnering with families to learn about care practices, expectations, and values of young children's home cultures. They also honor and respect the information they learn about babies to inform their daily routines. Current professional understandings of care and education for very young children come mainly from Western research and prevalent

Euro-American practices (Bhavnagri & Gonzalez-Mena, 1997). We also need to recognize the diverse backgrounds that families and babies bring to early childhood settings. What if infant–toddler teachers come upon a difference between the expected daily practices that the program values and the child-rearing practices of the families? What if the expected daily practices differ from the teacher's home cultural experiences and practices?

> *Milo, 14 months, is a new child in the classroom. During afternoon snack time, Erica (Infant Teacher) puts some small pieces of watermelon on the table and a fork in front of Milo. Milo uses his two fingers to grasp a watermelon piece and puts it into his mouth. Milo then grasps another piece and uses his index finger to press the watermelon, watching the juice come out of the piece. Erica gives Milo a fork. Milo holds the fork with his right hand and then reaches for the watermelon with his left hand. He squishes the watermelon piece with his hand, not eating it.*
>
> *Milo's mom, Kai, comes in to pick Milo up. Kai says, "Milo, we do not play with the food." Milo does not stop playing with the food. Kai says, "Milo, you should eat your fruits. We don't play with food. You gotta eat. Do you want a toy to play with?" Kai gives Milo the lid of the bowl to play with and starts feeding Milo watermelon pieces.*

Striving for independence is seen as an important accomplishment in Western cultures (Markus & Kitayama, 1991). In Milo's program, babies were encouraged to take part in the feeding process. Erica (Infant Teacher) put fruit pieces and a fork on the table for Milo to feed himself to support his independence and self-help skills. Erica's practice was in line with the program's goal. Milo, however, seemed very interested in exploring the food rather than eating it. He was perhaps using his senses and exploring how it feels to squish the watermelon in his hands and between his fingers. Exploring the food can be a step along the way to learning and building an interest in food. However, Milo's mom, Kai, was not feeling comfortable seeing Milo exploring food. Milo did not seem particularly interested in feeding himself. As shown in the anecdote, Kai gave a toy to Milo to play with during mealtime so she could spoon-feed him. Kai did not want to make a mess while Milo tried to feed himself. The caregiving practices at home were not aligned with the program's expected practices.

What do we do when infant–toddler teachers face the challenge that their daily practices, in line with professional guidance, are different from those of families? Do we stick to the program policy stressing self-help skills? How do we reconcile the discrepancy?

We have no simple answers to these questions. Standing firm on all policies and practices is too rigid and not culturally sensitive. We do not want to undermine families' efforts and cultural and individual values. Meeting the individual needs of babies and families is essential in supporting optimal

The Complex Role of Infant–Toddler Professionals

development. Yet, infant–toddler teachers cannot and should not always modify what they do whenever a parent asks them to. Child-rearing beliefs and practices vary widely across cultures. There are many ways to raise a baby. Decisions and perspectives about how to put babies to sleep, how to feed babies, or how to discipline babies may vary from culture to culture and family to family. Through open communication, teachers and families must work together to find a way to fully support babies' appropriate and meaningful developmental goals and needs.

Returning to Kai and Milo's story, Kai seemed uncomfortable about Milo playing with food. During their parent–teacher conference, Kai shared her cultural experience regarding food with Erica and explained why she worried about Milo not eating enough. In Kai's words,

> *Kids in my home city were always spoon-fed during their breakfast and lunch-time. In Vietnam, the habit of spoon-feeding is generally kept until the baby is 3 or 4 years old. Parents and caregivers in my home city almost always hold a baby less than 2 years old when they feed them, try to get them to sleep, or want to take them somewhere. Parents often force their kids to finish their meals. Many parents frequently distract their kids from their unwillingness to eat more by offering them an iPad, TV, or toys. "Just one more spoon" is a repeated statement they often tell their kids. Of course, another spoon will lead to an-other until kids finish the meal. Forcing a kid to eat is definitely not a good way. It did not help me when I was young. But if my baby is skinny and does not seem interested in eating like I did, I do not know whether I am strong enough to follow his lead. I really wondered what best practice I could do if I were in that case. Malnutrition is still a big concern in Vietnam, although the issue of lack of food has been gone for decades in most families.*

The case of Kai highlights a difference in caregiving between the program policy, which advocates self-feeding, and her cultural experiences. It is also very possible that Milo was not feeling hungry at that moment. As she grew up in a culture emphasizing eating enough, Milo playing with food and not eating was a struggle for Kai. Also, in some cultures, food is never a plaything. While taking the time to learn about families and their beliefs, values, and priorities, teachers may be able to find ways to support both Milo and Kai in the center. Milo can have utensils to work on and develop coordination skills. At the same time, the teacher can hold utensils to feed Milo from time to time to make sure he eats. We can also share our professional expertise and let Kai know that, like many adults, babies don't always eat the same amount at each meal or on each day. We must trust babies. Babies can make their choices and know when they have enough to eat. At the same time, it is a good idea to watch progress over time and see whether babies are healthy and continue to grow. If so, they are probably getting enough food to meet their needs. We can also communicate how self-feeding can be a significant developmental milestone and promote feelings of independence among babies.

Open communication and partnering with families can help teachers become more culturally sensitive and bridge possible differences in home life and early childhood practices. Doing so can enable teachers to avoid either/or approaches and still be professionals and share their expertise. Working with diverse families requires cooperation and compromise rather than contradiction (Recchia & Fincham, 2019). "Seeing more than one perspective is the goal of communication" (Gonzalez-Mena, 2001, p. 369), and different perspectives can complement, rather than contradict, each other (Recchia & McDevitt, 2018).

It is critical to work with families to understand diverse caregiving practices. It is also equally important to acknowledge that teaching is closely connected to teachers' prior lived experiences. The way teachers were raised, their family values, and their culture could influence their expectations of babies. As described below, Benilda felt tension every time she put the babies in a crib, leaving them to cry out loud to sleep independently. Her home cultural experiences did not fit well with the program's professional practices that she was seeing, observing, and learning in her practicum placement.

> *The practices back home (Philippines) are very different from that which I am learning during the practicum. The children are immediately attended to, and their needs are given almost instantly in all attempts to avoid crying. So, I was always nervous every time I put an infant in their crib. In my culture, we almost never leave the kids alone. Leaving a kid who is crying out loud made me feel unpleasant, and I kept asking myself what if the kid hurt themself. The practices I am accustomed to differ from what I am learning at the Center. Now, I actually see firsthand the effects of allowing the baby to cry a little—they learn to self-soothe.* (Benilda, Infant Practicum Student, Reflective Journal)

As Benilda mentioned in her reflection, she was able to negotiate her inner conflict and become open to new learning within the U.S. practicum program. In the same vein, Sharina reflected on how her practicum experiences supported her in appreciating different ways to empower young children.

> *Having the experience of working at a center in the United States has allowed me to appreciate the different ways in which caregivers empower their students and teach them without using power or total control over them. I was born and raised in the Dominican Republic, and back home all the schools have strict schedules and routines that are followed on a daily basis . . . I have been able to learn how important it is to allow babies to guide their own learning and to explore with materials and objects. It is true that as teachers we are responsible*

The Complex Role of Infant–Toddler Professionals 73

for managing our classrooms and setting the tone, however, when we include the students and we make them part of the process, they are able to understand and follow the rules and routines in a more appropriate way. At the Center, babies are empowered to develop their autonomy and to explore and manipulate objects according to their interests. There are routines in place, but each child follows a unique schedule according to their needs. (Sharina, Infant Practicum Student, Reflective Journal)

The issue of cultural sensitivity is more urgent now than ever before because the caregiving practices of diverse families differ from the prevalent European American practices (Gonzalez-Mena & Bhavnagri, 2000). Just as we do not expect parents to change their beliefs, teachers should not be expected to change their beliefs and values. Instead, teachers, especially those from diverse cultural backgrounds, should be given an opportunity and space to explore the conflicts between what they are accustomed to and what they are now learning. Creating a supportive space for infant–toddler teachers to reflect on their previous knowledge within the context of this new learning is critical (Gupta, 2006).

Promoting a sense of belonging for infants and toddlers in early childhood is essential. It is equally vital for infant–toddler teachers to feel a sense of belonging in their settings, which is fundamental to their overall well-being and that of the babies. The diverse lived experiences of both infant–toddler teachers and babies should be valued, embraced, and appreciated.

DISCUSSION QUESTIONS

1. How have you observed or felt love in caring for infants and toddlers? Do you see love as an essential part of your professional identity as an infant–toddler teacher?
2. What would you do if the expected daily practices at your site differed from your own cultural expectations and experiences?
3. What do you do to cope with the stresses that come up when caring for babies? For example, how would you respond to an overtired, crying baby who you have been trying to help to sleep for 15 minutes?
4. Thinking about your practice, what do you do to support diverse individual and cultural ways of being for infants, toddlers, and families?

CHAPTER 6

Becoming an Infant–Toddler Teacher
Ways of Thinking and Ways of Being

I think back to the beginning of the semester, and I was nervous about stepping into the practicum. I had no experience working with infants and toddlers. I am very happy that Marco has been my key child for this semester. He is a very interesting, loving, and adorable child. Working with him so closely has made me appreciate him so much, and I feel that I have learned how to build trust and a relationship with babies. The practicum provided me the opportunity to build relationships with other practicum students, head teachers, and my professor, and helped me to think carefully and critically about my practice every day in the classroom. I could have never anticipated how wonderful this experience would be. (Alyssa, Infant Practicum Student)

Infant–toddler pedagogy is complex and multifaceted. It takes time to come to understand how to teach and learn alongside such young children. The above anecdote illustrates how a student teacher experienced the various benefits of a primary care system for early childhood professionals working with infants and toddlers. Through primary caregiving, student caregivers have valuable and unique opportunities to build relationships with their key children as they work with other students and professionals within an infant–toddler practicum. Although experiences like these are recommended for preparing early childhood teachers to work with infants and toddlers, the opportunities to engage in direct, hands-on experience working with infants in early childhood teacher education programs are limited (Horm et al., 2013; Recchia et al., 2015).

Our aim in this chapter is to recognize the important preparation and support systems that are needed to better prepare early childhood teachers to enact high-quality and responsive care in diverse infant–toddler education and care settings. Relationship-based care provides a context for facilitating infants' and toddlers' optimal development. A primary care system is proposed as an essential framework to promote relationship-based care and provide continuity of care, which can be beneficial and emotionally enriching to both infants–toddlers and teachers. We discuss the value of integrating well-structured, field-based practica into teacher education programs

74

Becoming an Infant–Toddler Teacher

to develop observation skills, learn to see through babies' eyes, understand babies' cues and interests, and better communicate and be in sync with babies. We propose providing time and space for teachers to experience and build relationships with infants and toddlers to become more responsive practitioners. This chapter also speaks to the importance of implementing a multilayered support system, including ongoing supervision, mentoring, and peer co-reflection, as learning is a collective endeavor.

RELATIONSHIP-BASED CARE AND THE PRIMARY CARE SYSTEM

As we have reiterated throughout this book, prioritizing human relationships is critical in infant–toddler care and education. Infants and toddlers thrive from a base of loving relationships. As Shonkoff and Phillips (2000) argue, "relationships, and the effect of relationships on relationships, are the building blocks of healthy development" (p. 27). Infants' and toddlers' development and learning occur in the context of early relationships with teachers who provide responsive, respectful, reliable, and trusted care (Gloeckler & La Paro, 2016). In addition to responsive caregiver–child relationships, the relationships among infant–toddler teachers, staff, and families are equally significant and should be honored (Recchia, 2016). Relationship-based care, therefore, has been highly recommended by numerous researchers and scholars to nurture infants' and toddlers' learning and growth and to ensure high-quality infant care and education (Degotardi & Pearson, 2014; Edwards & Raikes, 2002; Elicker et al., 2014; Lally et al., 2002; McMullen & Apple, 2012; Raikes, 1993).

A powerful way to facilitate relationship-based care is a primary care system or key-person approach (Elfer et al., 2003; Lally et al., 2002; Margetts, 2005; McMullen & Apple, 2012; NICHD, 1996). As indicated in the opening anecdote and here again in the vignette below, a primary care system can be beneficial and emotionally enriching for babies, primary caregivers, and parents:

> When I was first introduced to this key child–key caregiver idea, I was thinking, how does that work? I questioned that at the beginning. Throughout the semester, I learned that it really gives you one child to focus on, and you get to develop a warm relationship with one child, such as my key child, Amy. Being a key caregiver, obviously, you are gonna take a bigger interest in your key child in learning about them, but not necessarily be the only one person who answers all questions for and about the child. I think the key child–key caregiver is a good idea. It's a really helpful thing both for the kids and for us as caregivers. I feel really good about working with Amy's parents. I've gotten to know them and meet them many times and talking with them on a regular basis helps me get to know Amy and feel closer to Amy. (Lucy, Infant Practicum Student)

As described by Lucy, a key caregiver approach might be novel to some teachers within teacher education programs and early years settings. As Lucy (and many others) might ask, how does it work? A primary caregiver or "key" person is a specially assigned teacher who is primarily responsible for, works with, and cares for a specific child we refer to as a "key child." Only a few babies will be assigned to the key caregiver. The key caregivers become the "resident experts" on their key children and work closely with other caregivers and liaise with families. Although other caregivers will also interact with and care for all of the children in the room as needed, the key caregiver will most likely get to know and understand that child and family best. In this way, a primary care system promotes the overall well-being of babies and a reciprocal relationship among a key caregiver, a key child, and family members.

A primary care system can be particularly valuable for babies new to a setting. The key caregiver can be the one who greets their key child in the morning, possibly every time the child comes to the setting. While providing continuity of care, the caregiver can support a smooth transition into and adaptation to a new environment for their key child. Having one caregiver take primary responsibility can help babies who are new to the environment be less anxious around separation from their parents (Page et al., 2013). In a busy infant room, it is also very possible for some infants and toddlers, especially those quiet and less demanding ones, to receive less attention from teachers. Primary caregiving can ensure that all young children receive special attention from their key caregivers. Each baby will have someone special, observing and being together with them. Each baby will have an opportunity to develop a relationship with at least one teacher in the setting, regardless of their background, personality, behaviors, or any other circumstances in their life. "Therefore, a primary care system can be a powerful way of bringing more equitable and socially just care to all infants" (Lee et al., 2016, p. 347). This special relationship can help babies feel confident to explore their surroundings more, play more, and form other relationships (Raikes & Edwards, 2009). A primary care system, in this sense, will facilitate infants' and toddlers' overall development and well-being (Margetts, 2005; Recchia, 2016).

Through primary caregiving, caregivers share authentic interactions with their key child. As caregivers spend more focused time getting to know and understand their key infant(s), they will be able to engage in a more meaningful and more individualized relationship. For caregivers, a close relationship with their key child can provide emotionally rewarding experiences. However, as Lucy mentioned, primary caregiving is not equal to exclusive care. Caregivers also need to work with and support other teachers as a team (Honig, 1993; Lee, 2006). Given the nature of infant–toddler group care and the long days that some babies spend in childcare, there is an essential need for team teaching. The staff must work closely to ensure the day-to-day practice is as smooth and consistent as possible. As infant–toddler caregivers gain richer understandings of the children in their care, their practice becomes more effective, individualized, and empowering, generating more opportunities for deeper learning (Margetts, 2005; Lee, 2006; Page, 2014).

Lucy also articulated how her partnership with families enabled her to understand and feel close to her key child, Amy. A primary care system can be viewed as a triangle of trust connecting child, parent, and key caregiver (Elfer et al., 2003). With the parents' help, Lucy can become more familiar with and tune in to Amy's needs. Parents, in turn, may feel reassured and confident about their child's experience of being well cared for in the childcare setting. Primary caregiving strengthens the family-school partnership and supports the development of trust between babies and their caregivers (Lally et al., 2010).

Forming responsive and respectful relationships is the hallmark of quality early care and education. Primary caregiving can offer unique and valuable opportunities to develop responsive caregiving in infant–toddler childcare and support teachers in becoming more sensitive and competent (Dalli, 1999; Honig, 1993; Lally, 2013; Lally et al., 2010; Margetts, 2005). Relationship-based care and primary caregiving are highly promising practices (Recchia, 2016) that should be incorporated into teacher education programs and implemented in childcare centers.

BEING WITH AND LEARNING FROM INFANTS AND TODDLERS

The skills required of infant–toddler caregivers are highly specific but often undervalued (Manning-Morton, 2006). There is no doubt that quality infant–toddler caregivers must possess broad theoretical knowledge, observation skills to understand and respond to babies' cues and interests, a disposition toward inclusivity, and an ability to engage in teamwork (Recchia et al., 2015). A well-constructed and supervised field-based practicum with infants and toddlers can provide valuable hands-on experience to future early childhood professionals. Through hands-on experience over an extended period of time, infant–toddler teachers gain highly specific and professional skills that promote relationship-based care.

Power of Observation: Learning to See Through a Baby's Eyes

Observation is crucial to understanding babies' learning and development and, more importantly, the basis of a responsive pedagogy. Infant–toddler teachers get to know babies by carefully watching them, interpreting what we see and hear babies doing and saying, and being responsive to their needs during interactions (Howes & Hamilton, 1993; Recchia & Shin, 2010). The

78 Creating Interpersonal Environments That Support Responsive Care

following vignette describes how observant Martha was as a caregiver and, as a result, how Elly and Martha have begun to establish a powerful social and emotional connection.

Elly, 5 months, lies on her blanket kicking her feet and smiling. Martha (caregiver) watches from a distance, responding each time Elly vocalizes or coos. "I see you are kicking fast today, Elly! You really seem to be enjoying yourself!" she says. Suddenly Elly stops making happy sounds and begins to fuss. She squirms a little as she looks toward her caregiver. Martha approaches and reaches out to her. She asks Elly, "Do you want to come up?" as she waits for her to extend her arms in agreement. As Martha holds and gently rocks her, Elly calms and nestles into her shoulder. Soon Elly opens her mouth and begins to suck on Martha's shoulder. "Shall we get your bottle? It looks like you are hungry!" she says.

Communication skills among infants are still emerging. Careful observation is thus key to understanding their unique ways of communicating and being with others. As shown in the anecdote, Martha has learned to observe Elly carefully to understand her communication system and her preferred ways of moving and exploring her environment. Elly has come to know that Martha will respond to her cues and can be relied upon to meet her needs. Martha was also speaking *with* rather than speaking for or to Elly. In the context of their growing relationship, Elly and Martha are learning to communicate socially and emotionally through interactions that promote reciprocal and synchronous connections (Shonkoff & Phillips, 2000). Establishing this emotional "intersubjectivity" (Trevarthen, 1979) provides a context for Martha and Elly to build a trusting relationship that will serve as the foundation for Elly's ongoing exploration and learning.

One approach to help caregivers hone observation skills and be responsive to babies is the "Watch, Wait, and Wonder" (WWW) philosophy (Muir, 1992). When guided by the WWW philosophy, caregivers get down on the floor with the baby, wait, and quietly and actively observe them. You will always follow the baby's lead without initiating activities or imposing your own agenda. Thus, you will be responsive to the baby's lead but not take over their activities. Babies will have the freedom to explore under your care. WWW is an approach designed to improve sensitivity and responsiveness and support a healthier caregiver–child relationship.

We are learning to see through the eyes of a child. I must say WWW philosophy is not as easy as I thought. In the beginning, I was confused because I didn't know how much I could interact with the child without taking over. But I learned to step back and observe. There was a time I was in the kitchen with Blake. She began playing with various utensils and plastic foods. I began to ask her what she was cooking and what she was going to do next. But I soon realized that my narrative and questions were not matching her actions or receiving responses. Blake was not creating the dramatic play scenario that I had in mind. After watching her for a few moments, I began to understand more of what she was doing, and she led me in a hide-and-seek game with the objects. This WWW philosophy was really helpful because I felt I knew the child better without actually initiating the interaction. (Emma, Infant Practicum Student)

This reflection highlights how using the WWW philosophy allows infants and toddlers to tell and show caregivers what they are doing and need. For example, when Emma approached Blake with her own conception of dramatic play, Blake did not respond. Only after spending time observing Blake could Emma take the child's point of view and see the world through her eyes in a very real way. As Emma articulated, observation is vital to seeing, hearing, and understanding babies and thus to sharing meaningful social interactions. Responding in this way nurtures infants' sense of themselves as valued, understood, and cared for.

Taking Time and Sharing Space

Relationships do not happen instantly or overnight. As we discussed in a previous section, caregivers must get to know infants and toddlers deeply and adapt their responses accordingly. This process involves time, space, and effort and requires repeated opportunities for being together in a supportive environment (Degotardi & Pearson, 2014; Lee, 2006; Raikes, 1993; Recchia et al., 2018). As Zhu shares in the scenario below, caregivers need to step back and take significant time and space to truly understand babies' interests, needs, and interaction styles.

My experience working with infants taught me the importance of staying back and taking my time to understand their needs in different moments. Every child has its own rhythm, style, and routine for doing things. I must remember this "dance" can be different with every child. It is very important for a caregiver to get to know them to understand their needs and dispositions. I placed myself near Mia (key child) so she can reach me when she needs to or so she can invite me to her game, but I was also at a distance and available for her. I respected her space and gave her freedom of movement. I also gave myself room to explore and learn how I can provide appropriate and effective support to the children. By watching children exploring and developing, I was exploring my roles and my space. (Zhu, Infant Practicum Student)

Zhu beautifully describes how important it is for infant–toddler teachers to take time and space to learn about babies and themselves in their care. The relationship-building process takes at least 6 to 8 weeks of regular, ongoing contact to develop (Lee, 2006). "Over time and with consistency,

80 Creating Interpersonal Environments That Support Responsive Care

the relationship among the primary caregiver, infants, and parents deepens" (Raikes & Edwards, 2009, pp. 81–82). Synchronous relationships not only take time but also involve effort and investment (Degotardi & Pearson, 2014). Merely spending limited time with or observing babies will not result in synchronous relationships. High-quality time with babies must be prioritized, invested in, and shared freely (Recchia & Fincham, 2019).

Additionally, as Zhu expressed, deep connections with babies emerge through the space of being with babies. Most importantly, although it might sound paradoxical, taking some distance from babies can promote close connections. When caregivers take this distance, they look beyond their own agenda and allow space for babies to be themselves and explore the world. Caregivers respect babies by being there for them and following their lead. This process allows caregivers to get to know each baby's rhythms, needs, and styles. Taking time and space enables teachers to establish a reciprocal, responsive infant–caregiver relationship, which has been described as an extended dance (Raikes & Edwards, 2009). Zhu also articulated a critical point: Teachers must take time and space to explore their roles and grow professionally within a supportive environment.

Supporting Culturally and Developmentally Diverse Expressions of Social and Emotional Communication

With population changes, more culturally and linguistically diverse infants and toddlers are entering early care settings. As culturally responsive caregivers, we need to pay attention to cultural diversity as we help provide continuity between home and childcare. One area of importance, for example, is learning about the child's native language since "the home language is a child's connection to the love, nurturing, and lessons learned in the family context" (Nemeth & Erdosi, 2012, p. 50). Having a child's family share a list of the words they are speaking at home can help caregivers be more in tune with a child's emerging language. Appreciating a child's communication capabilities and validating their cultural identity will help teachers to bridge a child's experiences between home and center, as illustrated in the anecdote below:

> Suhye, 15 months, is a happy child, always babbling and smiling. Suhye takes a few steps toward Jessica (caregiver), who is at the eating table. Suhye vocalizes "mamma . . . mamma." Jessica responds, "Hi, there." Suhye looks up to see Jessica. Jessica smiles at Suhye, and Suhye smiles back at Jessica. But Jessica does not pick Suhye up. Suhye then sits down, crawls to the fridge, and babbles "mamma . . . kka kka." Suhye finds pictures posted on the fridge and touches one picture of her family, saying "umma." Jessica looks at Suhye, saying "Suhye, you have a lot to say today." Marianne (head teacher) comes near Suhye and lowers herself a little to look at the picture, saying, "Who's there?"

Suhye looks up to see Marianne. Marianne now squats down, points to the picture and says, "Is that Umma (mommy)?" Suhye beams at Marianne.

Suhye's vocalizations were more than making random sounds. When you pay attention to the child's native language, Korean, Suhye's babblings were her deliberate attempts to communicate that she wanted to eat food (*mamma*) or snack (*kka kka*). Suhye's intention, however, was not read accurately by Jessica. Those communication efforts can be misunderstood or misinterpreted based on caregivers' language backgrounds and experiences. When Marianne used simple words, such as *Umma* (mommy) in Suhye's native language, Suhye felt more connected with Marianne. Suhye's smiling and beaming at Marianne suggest she was pleased with their encounter.

Individual characteristics can influence the development of relationships (Degotardi & Pearson, 2014). Some infants and toddlers feel comfortable playing close to one another, while others may feel the same space is too close for comfort. Some may use more subtle and physical cues rather than verbal cues. For example, Nom, an African boy, was a verbally quiet child with his parents, caregivers, and his peers. It was observed that his mother often relied on animated and nonverbal expressions in her interactions with him. Although he was observant of the environment and others' play, Nom used no words to communicate with others.

Nom, 24 months, picks up a big maraca and puts it into a large transparent tube mounted on the wall. The maraca is stuck in the middle of the tube. Felicia (caregiver) approaches and asks, "Nom, would you like help?" When Nom does not respond, Felicia taps his hand for his attention. When Nom looks at her, Felicia asks him again, tapping the tube. Nom imitates and taps the tube with Felicia. Nom moves to the other (low) side of the tube and sits on the floor, but he cannot take the maraca out. He reaches out his hand toward Felicia and points to the tube. She points the tube out to Nom two times and says, "You can try . . ." Felicia taps the tube harder, and Nom looks up at her and starts tapping the tube lightly . . . After one last hard bang, he walks away.

Nom faced a challenge in his play when the maraca got stuck in the tube. As shown, Nom had a very physical way of engaging with others. He would use a range of facial expressions and occasional sounds to communicate his feelings and interests. During the morning drop-off time, Felicia noticed that Nom and his mother often relied on more animated facial expressions to communicate rather than verbal interactions. Honoring his preferences and communication styles, Felicia utilized multiple strategies to engage Nom. For instance, Felicia asked him verbally, made physical contact with him by tapping his hand, and then tapped on the tube asking him again if he wanted help. Felicia assumed that Nom had something important to communicate, and she demonstrated through her responsive actions how this kind of highly responsive caregiving can be critical to reading babies' subtle and nonverbal cues accurately. Teachers must adapt their ways of interacting with babies to support the diverse communicative styles enacted within different languages and cultures. Recognizing and honoring cultural, linguistic, and ability diversity is a fundamental component of working with young children and families (Derman-Sparks & Edwards, 2010).

Infant–toddler caregivers are often the first to become aware of developmental differences in young children's ways of being in the world. Paying careful attention to the nuances of development can help them to better assess children's learning and potential and communicate with families about what they are observing (Recchia, 2016). Teachers who have a firm understanding of early development are better positioned to help families seek out special education services if needed and navigate the complexities of the referral process.

Early childhood teachers who lack a background in special education may express initial concerns about their ability to adequately meet the needs of children with disabilities (Recchia & Lee, 2004). However, over the years we have documented much success in creating inclusive infant–toddler environments that focus on honoring diversity and uncovering children's strengths through relationship-based practice (Recchia et al., 2022; Recchia & McDevitt, 2023).

Primary caregivers who are assigned key children with special needs may find that these children are more dependent on them for care and interaction than their typical peers, especially as they are first establishing relationships with them. Caregivers need support and understanding as they work to create inclusive curricula and develop strategies for responding meaningfully to a variety of child needs. Administrative support for inclusion is essential to its success, as we discuss further in Chapter 7.

In infant–toddler classrooms, it is customary to see a wide range of skills and competencies among the children. Beyond achieving developmental milestones, individual children develop at their own pace; they may approach learning and exploration in very different ways. Infant–toddler caregivers need to think about ways to value and appreciate these individual differences, and to create inclusive environments that honor and respect children who may need extra support to fully engage in relationships with caregivers and peers that will facilitate and expand on their learning opportunities (Recchia & Lee, 2013).

BECOMING AN INFANT–TODDLER PRACTITIONER WITHIN A SUPPORTIVE LEARNING COMMUNITY

With Charlotte, for example, determining when to help her is a bit tricky, as she tends to cry and become fussy very easily; in some instances, it's better to let her

Becoming an Infant–Toddler Teacher

work it out on her own (and thus avoid carrying her around all day just to keep her calm!), but other times she really does need the comfort or assistance. But in general, I'm seeing that the more I get to know the personalities, strengths, and needs of the children, the easier it is to decipher these meanings. (Gabriella, Infant Practicum Student)

How do caregivers new to working with infants and toddlers come to understand and engage in quality practice with this age group? Early childhood teacher education programs across the nation offer little course content or practicum experiences related to infants and toddlers (Norris, 2010), and most childcare teachers enter the field with little preparation to work with them (Nicholson & Reifel, 2011). Infants and toddlers learn in ways that are different from older preschoolers, so a specialized understanding of teaching and learning is required for children from birth to 3 years. Child development courses may outline the basics of developmental milestones in infants and toddlers, but true understandings of what it means to engage in high-quality teaching and caregiving with this age group are much less straightforward (Recchia, 2016).

Value of Field-Based Experiences

As illustrated in the above scenario, Gabriella is learning to read Charlotte's cues through practice in everyday caregiving. When early childhood teacher preparation programs fail to provide teaching skills and supervised practice focused on infants and toddlers, they exacerbate the lack of comprehensive preparation to teach this age group, even among certified early childhood teachers (Beck, 2013; Horm et al., 2013; Ray et al., 2006). With few opportunities to experience the ways that early development comes to life in practice, knowledge about infancy often remains theoretical, academic, and superficial.

This lack of experience, coupled with ambiguous feelings about what it means to be an infant teacher (Beck, 2013; Rockel, 2009), can make students uncomfortable working with babies, and it often takes some time before they are able to fully immerse themselves in teaching and caregiving routines (Jung et al., 2021; Loizou & Recchia, 2018). Learning the highly specialized skills for providing responsive early care and education takes time and practice, and this process is not necessarily intuitive (Manning-Morton, 2006; Nimmo & Park, 2009).

As mentioned earlier, studies have shown that it takes at least 6 to 8 weeks of ongoing contact with infants in childcare before a caregiver–child relationship develops (Lee, 2006; Recchia & Shin, 2010). Through this relationship, quality responsive teaching and caring take place. *It is essential to be hands-on with babies to know and understand them, and it takes time to get connected and stay connected.* Yet it is often the case that the youngest children on the early childhood spectrum, infants and toddlers, receive the least amount of focus in preparation programs, even those that certify teachers from birth.

In our work with practicum students in infant–toddler settings, we have come to see how relationships must be felt to be understood. As discussed in the previous chapter, as student caregivers come to know and love the infants and toddlers in their care, they think differently about what babies need (Recchia et al., 2018). Quality field experiences allow those new to work with infants and toddlers the opportunity to learn to understand and engage in process quality, which happens "in process" and over time through the nuances of everyday life in infant and toddler rooms.

Professional Development for In-Service Teachers

At the beginning, I was stressed—what would I do if I had no plan? How would I help children learn and develop? How would I know the way the day would evolve? But then the children created games, I put out toys, and they naturally went to play with them, and I observed them. (Tina, PDP Video, Reflective Journal)

The professional development literature offers multiple strategies to support in-service teachers. Among them are training, observation/assessment, study groups, inquiry/action research, and mentoring. When teachers are new to working with infants and toddlers, however, first and foremost they need shared time and space with this age group and support to help guide their new understandings about teaching and caring in process. Tina, quoted above, was a participant in a study that explored how in-service teachers new to working with infants responded to a professional development program (PDP) designed to help them reenvision their practice (Loizou & Recchia, 2018). Like many early childhood teachers, Tina considered preparing materials and planning activities as her main role, which is in line with what she had been taught about working with an older early childhood population.

When the in-service teachers in this study were initially asked about their philosophy in working with infants, they were able to report those components of quality infant childcare that we see in the literature. They emphasized responsive caregiving, learning through play, and allowing the children to explore the environment freely. However, when asked to record a video of an aspect of their practice they valued most to highlight their teaching, all of them selected a structured activity as a representation. In discussing these choices in their first focus group, their comments reflected a distinction between their expressed beliefs about infant teaching and learning and their practices.

> *The fact that I plan for activities and think of the necessary materials makes me feel creative and that I give to the children, that I am a professional and I help them develop. The role of the infant teacher is not just care but education as well, basically educare. I have the need to know that the children have learned something and that they have developed.* (Daphne, Focus Group 1)

Later in the PDP, the teachers were asked to engage in "quiet time" with children, enacting a form of the WWW philosophy mentioned above. They were specifically instructed to let the children guide them, and to be actively observant but to limit their overtly verbal responses. Although they found this activity uncomfortable at first, in the end it was fundamental to helping them see the critical value of observation in their practice. By allowing the infants' space to construct their own experiences, the teachers became hyper-aware of not only the children's capabilities but also of the need to re-evaluate their previous notions of what teachers needed to do to promote early learning.

> *Many times, we [infant teachers] have the need to plan activities that infants do not really need. We need to spend time daily to listen to infants and observe their needs . . . we need to differentiate between our needs as educators and the true needs of infants.* (Athena, Conversational Interview)

Providing opportunities for in-service teachers new to infant–toddler teaching such as those described in this study can be instrumental in helping them reconceptualize their teacher identities.

Learning to Work as a Team

In addition to developing new notions about teaching and caring for infants and toddlers, teachers new to work in infant childcare may also need to learn new ways of working closely with other caregivers and with families. While teaching older students often takes place in one's own classroom, working with infants in groups is by necessity a collaborative enterprise. When infant–toddler teachers establish positive working relationships with families and colleagues, they add substantively to high-quality care by enhancing their knowledge of infants' needs and orchestrating more continuous caregiving throughout the day.

This essential component in infant–toddler teaching does not always come naturally to early childhood teachers, who are often drawn to the field because of their interest in working with children (Recchia, 2016). New

86 Creating Interpersonal Environments That Support Responsive Care

teachers are frequently surprised by the challenges they encounter in the field in their necessary collaborations with adults (Recchia & Beck, 2014). Administrators and mentors can provide support for embracing teamwork by making time for group discussion, team meetings, and reflective supervision at their centers.

Reflective Practice

> Given this week's topic of challenging behaviors, I have definitely been focusing on how my own subjectivity determines my handling of certain situations. The readings talked a lot about how subjective our reactions as caregivers are in situations of challenging behaviors, and this is something I've realized from the beginning of the course and have tried to be cognizant of. I know I have my certain "hot buttons," as we spoke about earlier in the semester, and so I try extra hard to be aware of when my reactions to certain situations are actually appropriate, or whether I am unfairly imposing my "issues" on the child. (Madeline, Infant Practicum Student)

We have underscored throughout this book that observation and reflective practice are critical skills, especially for infant teachers, because they enable teachers to gain greater insight into individual infants' characteristics and to respond to infants in more relevant and authentic ways (Recchia & Loizou, 2002; Recchia & Shin, 2010). Other researchers have also articulated the importance of providing space for infant educators to reflect on the pedagogical principles that guide their work with infants and toddlers (Elfer & Page, 2015). Elfer and Dearnley (2007) described a professional development program that allowed infant educators opportunities to express and reflect on their feelings, highlighting "the emotional complexity of their work" and suggesting that "provision for reflective space needs to be built in as an institutional requirement" (p. 278).

Reflection has also emerged as a critical piece in the learning process. Practicum experiences are enhanced significantly when preservice teachers are encouraged to simultaneously engage in reflective practices, such as keeping a teaching journal, engaging in frequent classroom observations, and raising questions about the children, teaching practices, and curricula they encounter in the field (Darling-Hammond, 2006; Recchia et al., 2009). As Madeline describes in the above anecdote, she is learning to tune in to her own emotional responses to the children, especially those that may be triggered in stressful negotiations with them.

In our previous work with new teachers, we have found that those experiences that pushed them to question their beliefs, such as engaging in a reflective journaling process with their supervisors, were most powerful in changing their thinking, echoing Dewey's (1998/1933) statement, "as long as our activity glides smoothly from one thing to another . . . there

Becoming an Infant–Toddler Teacher

is no need for reflection" (p. 14). Disorienting events or dilemmas, or the culmination of disorientating experiences over time, seemed to foster more reflection and transformative learning (Cranton, 2006; Mezirow, 1997). Without critically examining their experience and knowledge, teachers may get into repetitive patterns and "ignore or distort new ideas and practice" (Feiman-Nemser, 2008, p. 698). They need to bring their "implicit" and "tacit knowledge" (Cochran-Smith & Lytle, 1999, p. 263) to the surface by articulating it so that they recognize their own assumptions and beliefs.

In our studies, we found that new teachers who were prepared to use reflection as a tool during their preservice program brought this skill into their ongoing practice (Recchia & Beck, 2014). They used the reflective process to guide them in multiple ways. One participant used reflection to assess emotional responses to children:

> *[Reflection helps in] recognizing my own feelings when working with a child who is throwing a tantrum, because it affects me emotionally. And, yeah, you as a teacher, you want to prepare the children and help them recognize their feelings, but I need a lot of that myself. And so, I'm always aware of how I'm feeling . . . but it's like . . . think before you act . . . and be creative with solutions. Don't feel like there's one way to handle a situation . . . sometimes just changing a little thing could make all the difference. With one child, I kind of stumbled at first, but then through [reflection], I learned how to work with him. And it's changed our relationship.* (First-Year Teacher Interview)

Another shared how reflecting on her practice helped her to better process the details of what was happening in her classroom and make meaningful changes in her teaching:

> *Reflections. I hated them in grad school . . . I would always say, "Why do we always have to reflect so much on all this?" But this year I did the reflecting (for) 3 months because I realized the first day going in, there were so many things going on and I couldn't process it, so I had to write it down afterwards or during the day . . . I think it's . . . really what saved me because, looking back, I was able to look back at repetitive things that kept happening with the kids . . . and I was able to fix it the next time.* (First-Year Teacher Interview)

And another participant reported that the reflective process helped her to clarify and stand firm in her own beliefs:

> *I think that with the constant reflecting that we did, I was able to articulate my philosophy of education and I think that helped me become more confident. And I may have done things that were not status quo and, you know, maybe my principal or my colleagues would question, but because I reflected so much,*

I felt a little more secure and didn't question myself as much when other people questioned me. (First-Year Teacher Interview)

Given the demands of teaching and caring for infants and the complexities of working with diverse learners and their families (Recchia & Shin, 2012), reflection is a competency that can be applied broadly in infant teaching. Reflecting on emotional encounters with children and families is equally important to reflecting on philosophical beliefs that inform particular teaching practices, and both forms of reflection are associated with responsive pedagogy (Dalli et al., 2011; Recchia, 2016).

A Need for Mentoring and Peer Co-Reflection

Having an experienced, responsive, and intuitive mentor teacher or supervisor to help guide infant–toddler caregivers in their practice can be invaluable and is especially important in the process of preparing new infant–toddler teachers for the field (Recchia et al., 2015). Establishing a framework for enacting reflective practice in the context of an infant practicum has been an essential component in our work with preservice early childhood teachers. As caring for infants and toddlers in group care settings almost always happens in a collective environment, it is also important to create opportunities for peer co-reflection, which may call on a different set of skills.

One way of bringing these ideas to life within the context of teacher preparation is to create multiple opportunities for peer sharing among practicum students. Arranging for pairs of students to visit each other's sites as observers, for example, helps to give student teachers a better sense of their peer's experience, which supports a more meaningful co-reflection process as students come together in their practicum course. Peer pairs can also engage in responding to each other's reflective journal entries to provide additional feedback and support for their practice. Engaging with these tools for collaborative learning as part of professional preparation lays the groundwork for graduates to take these practices with them into the field (Puig & Recchia, 2008; Recchia & Puig, 2019).

Goouch and Powell (2013) discuss the power of professional dialogue among infant teachers not only in improving practice but also in transforming their sense of professional values and identity. Other researchers have documented the ways that collaborative meetings among infant–toddler professionals contribute to critical reflection on their fundamental beliefs and knowledge that can change their dispositions and practice (Swim & Isik-Ercan, 2013). Taken together, what grounds these professional development programs is a deep faith in the power of teacher knowledge, reflection, and collaboration in professional learning (Jung et al., 2021).

The reflective process can be further enhanced within a community that shares common goals when participating colleagues have differing views and experiences (Cochran-Smith & Lytle, 1999; Wenger et al., 2002). In these "communities of practice" (Wenger et al., 2002, p. 12), teachers come together to share their concerns, interests, and passions on an ongoing basis and to discuss, support, and challenge each other's knowledge, beliefs, assumptions, and practice (Puig & Recchia, 2008). Through this critically reflective process, teachers socially co-construct new knowledge and deepen their understandings and expertise.

In a study designed to explore the ways that student teachers in an infant–toddler setting engaged in collaborative practice at their practicum site, this sentiment was echoed (Jung et al., 2021). Weekly meetings for developmental goals and curriculum planning helped teachers become more insightful about the ways that infants and toddlers learn, make informed decisions on practice, and provide more intentional care and education for the children. The meetings also helped teachers form collegial relationship with their co-teachers and grow professionally through collaboration. As one participant shared,

> *Once we're able to discuss the children, then we can think about how to help their development. We do it better as a team because we all come with different ideas, and different aspects of the day . . . and children also form different relationships with different people.* (Jenny, Infant Practicum Student)

Jenny's comments reflect not only the value of this co-reflection process but the particular significance it has in the infant–toddler childcare setting. Because children may be present for more hours than their individual teachers, they will necessarily be cared for by multiple caregivers throughout the day. As Jenny articulates so clearly, each of these caregivers will have a different relationship with a particular child and may engage with them at different times of the day, affecting their experiences and behavior.

In infant–toddler childcare, it is natural to enact a coteaching model, where all teachers, regardless of their positions, become collaborative partners, taking "collective responsibility" (Roth & Tobin, 2005, p. 20), establishing common goals, planning and enacting curriculum, and evaluating teaching and learning (Gallo-Fox & Scantlebury, 2015, 2016; Murphy & Martin, 2015). Within this model of practice, teachers engage in "cogenerative dialoguing" (Roth & Tobin, 2005, p. 21) as a form of ongoing professional development, taking risks in experimenting with new possibilities as they enact changes in their practice. Successful coteaching works best when there is mutual respect, positive interpersonal relationships, and recognition of coteaching as a learning vehicle (Gallo-Fox & Scantlebury, 2015; Goodnough et al., 2009; Nilsson & Driel, 2010; Scantlebury et al., 2008).

In this chapter, we have discussed the value of implementing a primary care system to foster relationship-based care and enrich babies' and teachers' experiences. We articulated particular and professional infant–toddler teacher skills that promote relationship-based care. We argued that well-structured field-based experiences are an essential component of teacher education programs and a vehicle for helping new student teachers become more responsive practitioners. We emphasized that observation and reflection are an integral part of the learning process. Finally, we have shared some of the ways that a multilayered system of support can help teachers become collaborative partners, taking "collective responsibility" for their work with infants, toddlers, families, and colleagues.

DISCUSSION QUESTIONS

1. Who were your caregivers as a young child? They were your first model of what adults can do for children. What do you do that is like them?
2. What were some of your initial feelings as you began to care for infants and toddlers?
3. Thinking about your practice, what do you do to enhance your relationships with babies, families, and colleagues?
4. Is primary caregiving addressed at your site? If not, what can you do to help create a better sense of continuity of care for infants and toddlers?
5. What role do observation and reflection play in your practice? How do they contribute to enacting responsive care?

CHAPTER 7

Constellations of Care
Building Caring Infant–Toddler Communities

How often do you go to places, and you pass the parents. I don't even know everybody in my building, and here I come and they're, "Hi, how are you?" and they're just, you know, really, I love it. I really—and he does too, and I feel I can go to work with peace of mind [laughs] of what's happening, and again, like I said, I feel like you guys have our backs. You're here for the kids and everything for the kids, you know . . . you're as concerned about them as we are. (Bianca, Toddler Parent)

In this chapter we explore the ways that relationship-based practice can serve as an overarching framework to create and support caring childcare communities beyond the everyday social experiences in the infant or toddler room. Interjecting examples from practice throughout the chapter, we articulate a philosophical stance that holds all human relationships in high esteem, not only within early education practices but also in working with families, supporting staff, and creating administrative policies within an infant–toddler childcare environment. Intentionally infusing an ethic of care into both policy and practice decisions is at the core of responsive childcare and serves as a guide for both authentic teaching and learning and building meaningful family-professional partnerships. Critical elements within a caring community include policies for welcoming and supporting diverse children and families as they transition through the phases of childcare, and an openness to including children with unique ways of knowing, learning, and communicating. A focus on nurturing well-being in all members of the community honors a reflective stance and a commitment to listening and responding to multiple voices and points of view when challenges arise. In keeping with the non-prescriptive approach that undergirds the book, rather than proposing specific solutions to the issues addressed in this chapter, we provide examples of reflective thinking in particular situations that prioritizes honoring relationships and fostering community.

CONSTELLATIONS OF CARING/ETHIC OF CARE

Nel Noddings (2002) has elaborated on the ways that teaching and learning grounded in an ethic of care can transform experience within educational environments. Caring for others entails both being open and receptive to another's ideas while also demonstrating acts of caring as you relate to each other. As you have read in previous chapters, these ideas have been described as foundational aspects of high-quality early care and education for infants and toddlers. But to provide the highest level of quality, an ethic of care must undergird decision making across the center. Administrators, staff, and families all benefit from being cared for, and from caring for each other.

Overarching Philosophical Orientation Toward Prioritizing Human Relationships

We see quality care and education for infants and toddlers as grounded within a constellation of dynamic, caring relationships, mirroring connections among teachers and children; teachers and teachers; administrative staff and teachers; and teachers, staff, children, and families. A center's structural organization and policies, its philosophical approach to teaching and caring, its ability to provide ongoing mentoring and support to staff, and the leadership style it embraces come together in synthesizing the overall experience of quality care (Dalli et al., 2011; Recchia, 2016). Infant–toddler teachers and caregivers cannot be fully present with the children in their care if they do not feel supported themselves. When personal issues arise that may impact their ability to do their jobs as they would like, it's important that staff members know they are not alone.

> *Aida, a single mom and an infant caregiver, has been having a difficult time getting to work on time. Although her ex-husband is responsible for taking their daughter to school each morning, he does not always show up on time, leaving Aida in a tough position. If she must drop her daughter off at school, she cannot arrive on time for her shift in the infant room. Her supervisor is uncomfortable with the unpredictable schedule and is worried about coverage for the classroom in the early hours. Although she believes that Aida is an excellent caregiver who is loved by children and families alike, she knows it is not fair to the other workers who are having to pick up the slack when Aida is late. How can she continue to support Aida while also making sure the center runs smoothly?*

In some centers, Aida would most likely be given an ultimatum and perhaps eventually be fired for her tardiness. The rules about getting to work on time would take priority over any notions of honoring Aida's goodwill and her well-established ties with children, families, and staff at the center. Looking at this dilemma through the lens of prioritizing human

Constellations of Care

relationships, the first motivation would be to preserve the meaningful connections between Aida and others at the center. Although it might seem more difficult to problem-solve for a solution that can benefit everyone as opposed to simply following the rules, in the end everyone wins when we work together to find solutions that honor human relationships. Perhaps Aida can change her schedule; maybe she can find another parent at her daughter's school to do drop-off in exchange for something she can offer; or she might renegotiate with her ex-husband regarding their shared responsibilities. Helping Aida to find a solution that honors her as a valued colleague would take precedence when human relationships are prioritized.

A similar set of circumstances might apply with a family who is struggling to get their child to the center in the morning. Some parents find it especially difficult to negotiate with their toddlers during the rush of a busy morning. Managing a morning meal, dressing, packing lunches, and getting everyone out of the house when a feisty toddler refuses to get dressed or eat their breakfast can send the best laid plans into a tailspin.

> *Maggie, 22 months, is simply not a morning person. She hates getting out of bed, dislikes having to take off her favorite pajamas to get dressed, and prefers to ease into the day rather than be rushed to eat her breakfast quickly and get on the road to work and childcare. Her mother has become increasingly agitated with Maggie's morning resistance, while Maggie has begun to dig in her heels, adamantly refusing to comply. Her mother is embarrassed by Maggie's temper tantrums and feels uncomfortable forcing her to behave. This has created a great deal of drama at morning drop-offs.*

Stepping back to consider how to best provide support for Maggie and her mother through a lens of honoring human relationships requires thinking differently about the typical morning routine. Maybe Maggie can simply arrive at school in her pajamas and eat breakfast and get dressed there later when she is ready to jump into the busyness of the day. Chances are that taking the pressure off Maggie and her mother will relieve the tension that is fueling their struggle. Having a center director and/or a caregiver's support to allow this family to do things a little differently from the others sends the message that they are welcome and valued for who they are.

Seeing Families as the Primary Caregivers and Educators of Their Children

Just as we have described the importance of infant–toddler caregivers being emotionally available and responsive to the children in their care, these ways of being can also be applied to work with families. Respecting families as the primary caregivers and educators of their children, we seek and acknowledge their insights and understandings about their children's histories

94   Creating Interpersonal Environments That Support Responsive Care

and everyday lives. Infants' and toddlers' growing sense of themselves and the world they know emerges and is embedded within their family experiences. Through our relationships with families, we gain an enhanced understanding of children's expectations of being cared for and their responses to care (Gonzalez-Mena & Eyer, 2012).

> *Toshi, 12 months, is relatively new to childcare. Overall, he has adjusted well, except for his struggles with sleeping. Toshi's caregiver, Stacy, has followed the usual routines that work for the other children. But when she tries to put Toshi in a crib, he immediately becomes distressed and begins fussing, crying, and reaching to be picked up and held. In a conversation with his father, Stacy learned that their family custom is to sleep on special mats on the floor. Toshi has never been expected to sleep alone in a crib. This new knowledge helps Stacy understand Toshi's response in a different way and allows her and her co-teachers to develop a plan that honors his family's sleep experience. Allowed to sleep on a mat on the floor instead of in a crib, Toshi can rest more comfortably at the center.*

In this scenario, we see how input from Toshi's family has helped Stacy to think differently about his behavior. What could have been construed as Toshi being uncooperative is now seen as an appropriate response to a disconnect between his home culture and his center experience around sleeping. Making a small accommodation in Toshi's sleep routine to create continuity in his experience has made a big difference for his well-being. At the same time, gestures like these also honor families' beliefs and cultural practices and help form a bridge between home and center cultures.

> *Audrey, 15 months, always has the most meticulously prepared lunch in the infant room. Her mother, Mindy, has expressed to the caregivers that her daughter's health and nutrition are especially important to her. Mindy selects foods that she knows her daughter likes, and she expects her to eat what she prepares. The infant room philosophy supports young eaters by allowing them to make choices about what and how much they choose to eat. When Audrey leaves parts of her lunch unfinished, Mindy becomes upset with the caregivers. She tells them they should work harder to get Audrey to eat.*

When philosophies about what is best for young children differ between families and childcare staff, what can be done to continue to recognize parents as their children's primary caregivers and educators? Recchia and Williams (2006) discussed the importance of working within what Barrera and Corso (2003) call a "third space," or a place where different points of view are not only recognized but allowed to coexist. To honor families' belief systems, caregivers must think deeply about their own cultural identities, and the ways in which their program philosophies are grounded in a

Constellations of Care 95

particular worldview. Talking with Mindy about the program philosophy and inviting her to observe at mealtimes to see firsthand how the children respond might be a good starting point. The teachers might share their observations of Audrey's increasing success at self-feeding and her agency around food choices. Although it may not be possible to ensure that Audrey always eats all her lunch, the teachers can assure Mindy that they will continue to be mindful about not wasting her food. It might also be helpful for the caregivers to consider including some of the ways that Audrey is used to eating with her mother at center mealtimes. Not only would this be a way of honoring Mindy's beliefs, it would also provide continuity for Audrey between her home and school experiences.

Developing Family-Professional Partnerships

How do teachers negotiate differences between their own taken-for-granted beliefs and practices and families' expectations and ways of being with their children? Learning to communicate with families in a way that honors their knowledge and beliefs without compromising one's own professional expertise can be challenging at times. However, building authentic relationships with families is a primary step in providing quality care. As Cole and Lerner (2015) remind us, it's important to remember that families "have the greatest impact on their child's development"; the better infant–toddler teachers' relationships with families, "the greater the positive impact on children" (p. 1).

> Members of the infant room staff were worried that Kelly and John were too overprotective of their son Robbie, 17 months. A late walker, Robbie was just beginning to explore independently, and the caregivers were all about supporting his agency and motor development. They encouraged him to move on his own, believing he would learn best by taking small risks as he ventured into the larger world of the infant room. His parents, on the other hand, could not bear the thought of him falling or getting hurt in any way. Rather than encourage him to walk independently, they always held his hand and made sure the path was clear before he took steps. They expressed their concerns to the center director, who suggested they schedule a conference with Robbie's infant room caregiver.

Working from a place of empathy and respect, the conference might begin by simply listening to Robbie's parents' concerns. Robbie's caregiver can ensure that she communicates her openness to family contributions to their child's care, while at the same time sharing her observations of Robbie's success in learning to navigate the infant room. Providing assurance that safety precautions are always a primary concern in the infant room, she might invite Kelly and John to observe Robbie to see for themselves what she

96 Creating Interpersonal Environments That Support Responsive Care

believes he can do. This may be a topic for ongoing discussion between the family and caregiver, with continued check-ins about how things are going. Establishing a shared focus on Robbie's well-being can reassure his family that everyone has his best interest at heart.

Collaborative and authentic relationships with families can begin as soon as their children enter childcare by creating multiple opportunities for both formal and informal dialogue. Intake procedures such as an initial family meeting or a home visit can be special opportunities to get to know child and family preferences and values (Axtmann & Detweiler, 2005). When caregivers invite families into the infant or toddler room, establish a practice of daily communication, and ensure their availability for more formal meetings as needed, they lay the groundwork for strong relationships with families. Having these points of connection in place make it easier to tackle challenging situations should they arise (Croft, 2010).

VALUING INCLUSIVE PRACTICE/HONORING DIFFERENCES

Infant and toddler rooms are a natural environment for understanding and enacting inclusive education (Recchia, 2016). Although most infants and toddlers will follow a similar trajectory in mastering developmental milestones, they will not all move at the same pace. Some may stand out from the group in unique ways. When we welcome infants, toddlers, and families into an inclusive center community, we meet them where they are. Knowing that each child and family will come with their own "funds of knowledge" as well as individual and cultural ways of being allows caregivers to anticipate the diversity they bring (González et al., 2005).

True inclusion requires an openness to inviting everyone to the table and doing our best to support them once they arrive (Recchia & Lee, 2013). Initially a term used in special education to describe ways of working with children with disabilities within general education classrooms, *inclusion* has recently been used more broadly to encompass all forms of diversity such as cultural and linguistic diversity, neurodiversity, and developmental diversity. A center that values inclusion demonstrates this in its practices, from everyday routines and rituals to more formal administrative policies.

There may be many practical reasons for building a community of like-minded families by intentionally excluding those who are assessed as a poor fit for the center's philosophy and practices, such as reducing potential disharmony that might create challenges for the center staff. A truly inclusive center opens its doors to all they can accommodate, taking on potential challenges as they arise. Valuing inclusion requires a commitment to honoring differences and enacting practices that reflect a deep acceptance of and support for diversity.

Constellations of Care

Addressing Challenges That Arise in Curricular Decisions

When 2-year-old Carlos entered the toddler room, his parents expressed concerns about his eating and sleeping but did not note any worries about his development. The caregivers quickly noticed that his play was very ritualistic and, although he babbled, he did not seem to use any clear words in either Spanish (his home language) or English. He had a difficult time transitioning and cried on and off for weeks. He was occasionally interested in watching his peers' activity, but he did not engage them or join in their play. He did, however, take a lot of pleasure in activities involving music and movement, and was developing an attachment to a Spanish-speaking assistant teacher.

Carlos's primary caregiver suspected he might be on the autism spectrum but wanted to observe him carefully to learn more about his interests and ways of engaging before calling a conference with his parents. During the conference, she was able to share anecdotes describing Carlos's strengths as well as his learning differences and engage his parents in a discussion of his play and learning activities at home. She also invited his parents to observe Carlos in the toddler room and introduced the idea of referring him for an early intervention (EI) evaluation, emphasizing that the ultimate decision would be theirs to make.

In some infant–toddler programs, Carlos might simply be referred to special education without considering an inclusive approach. Many early childhood educators believe they are not prepared to work with children with disabilities; administrators often feel that the details of coordinating services and providing extra support would be difficult and time consuming. Staff members are often concerned that having a child with special needs in the program will take attention away from the other children (Barned et al., 2011).

In Carlos's inclusive program, there was no question about his leaving the center. Instead, the staff and the family worked together to find the best way to welcome and support Carlos in the toddler room. His parents decided to make a referral for evaluation, and he did qualify for EI services. A specialist began to visit the classroom several times a week to work with him alongside his caregivers and peers. Finding ways to capitalize on his strengths as they supported his play and relationships with adults and peers became the core curriculum for Carlos.

Addressing Challenges in Interpersonal Communication

Before starting in childcare, Lily, 14 months, was cared for primarily by her maternal grandmother (Chun Li). Chun Li came to the United States from China shortly after Lily was born to help her daughter, Ting (Lily's mother), who was returning to work after her maternity leave. Chun Li was very involved in Lily's transition to the center a few weeks earlier, and often spent extended time in the infant room at morning drop-off. She spoke only Cantonese, so communication with the English-speaking caregivers was challenging. Although they did not understand the words Chun Li was saying as she interacted with Lily and the other children, they were uncomfortable with her loud tone and what seemed like a harsh way of speaking. They expressed their discomfort to their supervisor, noting that they felt she was interfering with their ways of teaching and caring for Lily and the other children in the room.

When an infant–toddler program welcomes and prioritizes diversity, it is essential that both caregivers and administrators increase their levels of cultural awareness and cultural competency to be able to engage in caregiving partnerships with all kinds of families (Barrera & Corso, 2002). Children of immigrant families are the most rapidly growing segment of the U.S. population, making infants and toddlers in care settings increasingly more diverse (Murphey et al., 2013). However, infant–toddler caregivers, steeped in their own family and professional cultures, may not always be aware of or sensitive to diverse cultural practices (Banerjee & Luckner, 2014). Issues of equity and social justice can easily arise when early care professionals, often unknowingly, discount diversity in their compliance with "best" practices (Recchia & Shin, 2012; Recchia & Williams, 2006).

In the case of Lily, several elements may be contributing to the challenges in interpersonal communication between the infant room caregivers and her grandmother. Although it is difficult to fully overcome a language barrier, communication with families goes well beyond verbal language. Finding a way to include Chun Li as a contributor in Lily's childcare experience seems particularly important given her role as a primary caregiver during Lily's first year of life. Perhaps Ting, Lily's mother, who is bilingual, could help interpret in a joint meeting designed to learn more about Lily through Chun Li's eyes. It is also important for the staff to see Chun Li through both Lily's and Ting's eyes by observing the ways they interact with each other. Often what may feel inappropriate or uncomfortable in one culture is not so at all in another (Recchia & Williams, 2006).

RESPECTING AND SUPPORTING NEW AND CONTINUING TRANSITIONS

Infant–toddler childcare settings can be overwhelming at first for children and families new to center childcare (McDevitt & Recchia, 2022). Most infant and toddler rooms have several caregivers working alongside each other, and children may range from as young as 6 weeks to 3 years old, depending on center policies and state regulations. In some centers, there are clear separations in the grouping of young infants (pre-walkers or even pre-crawlers) and older infants who are more mobile. Toddlers may also be divided between younger and older groups. The greater the number of separate age groupings at a center, the more transitions will be required for the children and families who attend. Each time a child is required to change to a different care room, continuity of care can be disrupted as new relationships between children, caregivers, and families must be formed.

Welcoming New Children and Families to Childcare

At the Center for Infants, Toddlers, and Families (CITF), there is a gradual entry process. Infants and toddlers are divided into two rooms—one for infants 2 to 24 months, and one for toddlers 22 to 38 months, allowing some flexibility. Only a few children start during the first week, so caregivers can spend more time with them and welcome them individually to the center. Parents are invited to come into the classroom with their children, and gradually leave for longer periods as their children seem ready to engage in play.

How children and families are welcomed into a childcare setting can have a lasting impact on their adjustment and sense of belonging over time. It is also a reflection on the center's philosophical orientation toward inclusion, family- and child-centered practice, and relationship-based care (McDevitt & Recchia, 2022). At the CITF, all new families are invited to participate in a meeting with their child and the staff member who will be their primary caregiver, either at the center or during a home visit. Inviting families to talk about their children lays the foundation for shared caregiving. Not only is there a gradual start at entry, it is also staggered, with a few children starting at a time, so that the groups slowly build to their full size over the first few weeks. The transition process is individualized for each child and family, with some needing more than a week to become comfortable enough for full-time care in a new setting. This way of entering also allows the staff to address any special adjustment needs a child might have, and to spend more time with each new child and family. From the start, the groundwork is laid for a continued focus on child and family well-being.

Navigating Transitions Into and Out of the Infant or Toddler Room

Some families may find the gradual entry process to be cumbersome and inconvenient. They are anxious to get their children safely into childcare so they can go to work without worry. Having to take time off to be with their infants or toddlers through the process isn't possible for everyone. Most programs that engage in gradual entry allow another caregiver to be present for the process, such as a grandparent or babysitter who is close to the child, which can help to ease the burden. Thinking about this through a relationship-focused approach to infant–toddler care, we emphasize the critical importance of investing time and presence in the process of building the initial bonds among children, families, and center caregivers.

When it is time for a child and family to move to the next designated age group, a similar group change process can lay the foundation for a smoother transition. Each child and family adapts to change at their own pace (Recchia & Dvorakova, 2012, 2018), and providing support for flexibility around transitions is key to facilitating the new relationships that will unfold. Creating a formal process for checking in with families post-transition generates a space for communication and responsiveness to children's and family's needs and provides caregivers with information that can enhance their ability to build meaningful relationships.

CAPITALIZING ON OPPORTUNITIES TO BUILD COMMUNITY AMONG STAFF, CHILDREN, AND FAMILIES

Infant–toddler childcare settings often provide a culturally and linguistically diverse context where children, families, and the childcare staff make important social connections (Miller et al., 2014). Coming together so early in young children's lives provides an opportunity to start at the beginning, when foundations for future educational experiences are still being built. Teaching and caring enacted as a joint enterprise between caregivers and families, where everyone is welcomed to the table, different perspectives are honored and embraced, and individual differences are viewed as contributions as opposed to deficits can provide a powerful network of support within a childcare community.

New to the city and far from family and friends, Maya and her partner Chloe were eager to find childcare for their 8-month-old daughter, Daria, before starting their new jobs. As a nontraditional family, they were looking for a center that would welcome them as both parents and partners. They hoped to make connections with other families with infants to develop a social network and make new friends.

When infants and toddlers enter out-of-home care, their families become part of a community that extends beyond their home environment. They are invited to participate in special celebrations and are provided with a network of people to connect with when they need help or advice. The oft-used child-rearing adage "it takes a village" addresses a family's need for external support systems, often provided by relatives and friends. Family-centered, relationship-based infant–toddler childcare centers can also become a context for building this kind of community.

In the past, childcare settings, particularly those of poor quality, have been viewed by some researchers and families as less desirable

Constellations of Care

environments for infants and toddlers than their homes (Bradley & Vandell, 2007). Over time, societal and economic changes have shifted family priorities. Many young families have no automatic support system in place despite their need to work away from home. Research on early relationships has also broadened our understandings of infant–toddler social capacities (Davis & Degotardi, 2015; Singer & de Haan, 2007), highlighting the value of relationships beyond the mother–child dyad. Looking through a lens of relationship-based care, we see many benefits for children being cared for by a community of families, peers, and early care professionals as they form attachments to multiple caregivers and friendships with their peers (Howes & Hamilton, 1992, 1993; Howes & Ritchie, 2002).

Using Relationship-Based Practice to Guide Staff and Family Development Opportunities

The CITF closes 2 hours early each Friday, allowing a designated space for the full staff to come together. The time is used for both formal and informal professional development, sharing challenges and accomplishments in individual classrooms, and working together to solve issues or problems that arise. It is also a time to celebrate special occasions like staff members' birthdays, and simply to make more personal connections with each other. The director has encouraged families to help each other with early pick-ups and has provided a list of trusted babysitters and their contact information. Space is available to care for children on site if needed.

In addition to the benefits to children and families, infant–toddler caregivers who practice in settings defined by a strong sense of community support are more likely to invest in their work. Bussey and Hill (2017) describe the network of relationships formed by teachers and staff within childcare settings as a space for continued professional development, as they create a "community of practice," where they learn, create curriculum, and construct understandings of the children together. However, when structural supports are not in place to nurture the relationship process, higher stress levels for both infants and teachers can result (Shonkoff, 2010). Administrative support for what Dalli et al. (2011) refer to as "a membrane of supportive connections" (p. 89) requires employment conditions that encourage staff to feel valued and decrease teacher turnover; recognize the specialized nature of infant and toddler teachers' work; and encourage teaching practices that reduce environmental stress for infants (Thompson, 2016).

Although many programs prioritize accommodating family work schedules, doing so without considering the impact on professional development and community building for staff may ultimately compromise childcare quality. Infant–toddler childcare centers like the CITF see the caregiving staff as a vital component of the community, who must be nurtured professionally just as they nurture children and families. By embedding designated time and space for this practice into the schedule on a regular basis, the CITF communicates to families from the start that all members of the community must work together to sustain quality relationship-based childcare. Supporting the staff in this way also creates opportunities for families to share the responsibility and take part in the process.

MAKING ADMINISTRATIVE AND POLICY DECISIONS THAT REFLECT RELATIONSHIP-BASED PRACTICE

Engaging in relationship-based care begins with a deep commitment to a set of policies and practices that reverberate throughout an infant–toddler childcare program. A strong underlying philosophy and a set of principles that guide decision making are essential components in supporting children, families, and caregivers within a caring, responsive community (Recchia & Fincham, 2019).

> *At the CITF, families are surveyed regarding the most convenient times and the topics they are most interested in discussing during group parent meetings. They are asked if there is anything from their own family culture they would like to share with the children and staff. Several social events are planned to bring children and families together throughout the year, such as pot-luck dinners and a summer picnic. Interested families are welcomed into the classrooms to participate in weekly music time with the children or to share family rituals.*

Enacting family-centered, responsive, and culturally sustaining infant–toddler childcare asks a lot of administrators, caregivers, and families. It begins with a program philosophy that embraces sharing the care and education of infants and toddlers as a community by allowing multiple perspectives to inform practice. What professionals have learned is important for children may not be prioritized by their families. Inviting families as full participants in the childcare community requires that caregivers be able to suspend their personal beliefs at times to consider other perspectives. They must also find ways to convey their own knowledge and expertise in ways that do not disenfranchise families' beliefs and ways of being in the world.

Negotiating shared understandings about what is most important in the context of infant–toddler childcare happens best within authentic relationships grounded in interpersonal connections. Creating a childcare community that invites social connections among children, families, and staff lays the foundation for more meaningful connection and communication. These

Constellations of Care

human connections support greater openness to understanding differences and learning from each other (Recchia & McDevitt, 2018).

Becoming an Advocate for Children and Families

Nate, 18 months, and Brian, 19 months, have been peers in the infant room for over a year. They seek each other out as preferred playmates throughout the day, sharing similar interests in materials and activities. Although they have always played well together, just last week Brian bit Nate during what started as a playful interaction. Nate's parents became very upset when they were told of the incident and saw the bite marks on Nate's shoulder. They immediately called for a conference with the head caregiver and the director, demanding that Brian be expelled from the program.

Unexpected challenges can arise in a diverse childcare community when multiple perspectives create disagreements regarding policies and practices. In the case of Nate and Brian, how do the center's staff members consider all perspectives in finding a solution to this pressing dilemma? Nate's parents have a right to be upset that their child was bitten, and it's important to let them know they are heard and understood. However, it is also important to help them stand back from their emotional response in the moment to see the bigger picture. Nate and Brian have been together in childcare since their early infancy, and they continue to choose each other as playmates despite the altercation. The infant room caregivers have developed a plan for shadowing and redirecting Brian to circumvent his biting. Reiterating the center's policy on fostering inclusion and community, the director can step up as a leader in modeling this practice, letting Nate's parents know that children are never expelled from the program.

Advocating for children and families can lead us to spaces of contradiction where there are not clear answers about what is right or wrong. It may take time, careful attention on the part of the caregivers, and an openness to ongoing communication to allow the staff and Nate's family to move beyond the tension created by their different points of view (Recchia & Fincham, 2019). Ultimately, a compromise may need to be reached. Coming to a clearer understanding of what is fair from each perspective is a first step toward achieving greater harmony.

Looking Through the Lens of Possibility in the Face of Constraints

Infants and toddlers deserve to have "privileged relationships with caring adults" (Petrie & Owen 2005, p. 23), not only in their families but in their childcare settings as well. To develop and sustain these essential caring relationships, infant and toddler teachers must be supported by what we call "constellations of caring," or an overarching relationship framework, within the context of infant childcare (Goouch & Powell, 2013; Lee et al., 2016; Recchia, 2016; Recchia et al., 2015). Although ample research supports sensitive and responsive caregiver–child relationships as the most critical context for infant and toddler learning and development (Howes & Ritchie, 2002; Lally, 2009; NICHD Early Child Care Research Network, 2001; Raikes, 1996; Shonkoff & Phillips, 2000), less attention has been given to the importance of honoring all the relationships that need nurturing in an early care and education setting for infants, toddlers, and families (McMullen & McCormick, 2016; Recchia, 2016).

Envisioning a world where responsive, relationship-based, family-centered infant–toddler care and education is available to all families who choose it, we look through a lens of possibility. We see how caregivers and families work together to provide the most optimal care and education possible for the dynamic communities they form during this distinct time in families' and children's lives. Through creating a network of relationships that can continue to grow and change over time in response to children's changing needs, caregivers, families, and children continue to inspire and be inspired by their shared social environment (Degotardi & Pearson, 2009).

DISCUSSION QUESTIONS

1. Can you think of a time when you felt administrative support (or a lack of support) for an issue you were dealing with at your site? What happened and how did it get resolved?
2. How do you respond when you disagree with a curricular policy that is being imposed on your practice?
3. Thinking about your practice, how do you support children and families as they transition into the center or from one classroom to another?
4. How does relationship-based care contribute to your role as an advocate for infants, toddlers, and families?

CHAPTER 8

Enduring Reflections for the Field of Infant–Toddler Care and Education

In this chapter we offer a set of enduring reflections as a catalyst for re-imagining possibilities for the future of infant–toddler care and education. We reiterate the steadfast belief, grounded in scholarship and practice, that the capacity for human understanding and long-term social and emotional health and well-being emerge in the first few years of life within the context of reciprocal relationships, and that it is within these relationships that much of early learning takes place. We consider infants' and toddlers' rights to responsive and loving care, and the critical importance of creating caring environments that respect infants' ways of being and knowing in their own space and time. We further outline the ways that relationship-based practices can offer children and families in childcare a home for fostering community and subjective well-being. We return to the principles discussed in Chapter 1 to frame our visions for the future:

1. Human relationships are prioritized throughout the caregiving system.
2. Families are the primary caregivers and educators of their children.
3. Infants and toddlers are competent and innately motivated to learn.
4. An integrated, responsive curriculum strengthens infants' and toddlers' sense of self and their potential for learning and development.
5. Caregivers respect and appreciate infants' and toddlers' ways of being and sense of time.
6. Childcare centers foster community, belonging, and subjective well-being.

INFANTS AND TODDLERS AS BEING AND BECOMING

Although the literature abounds with information about the importance of the first 3 years of life as a critical foundation for all later learning and development (National Scientific Council on the Developing Child, 2007;

Shonkoff, 2010; Shonkoff & Phillips, 2000), not enough has been said about being with infants and toddlers in the everyday moments of their daily lives. The day-to-day routines and practices in childcare help to create what Lally (2013) calls a "social womb," where young children learn through responsive and supportive early relationships how to engage with others (Meltzoff & Kuhl, 2016), to understand the essence of their cultures (Recchia & Williams, 2006), to create their own theories of the world through play (Goouch & Powell, 2013), and to develop their attitudes toward learning. Through everyday interactions with others, infants and toddlers internalize a sense of who they are in the moment and begin to understand their own strengths and limitations (Thompson, 2016).

Rapid growth in learning and development during the first 3 years of life creates a dynamic space of encounter with caregivers and peers, which can change from day to day. Being in the moment with infants and toddlers allows caregivers to fully engage with them where they are today, creating continuity of experience through ongoing adaptations and responsive interactions as they grow and change (Jung & Recchia, 2013). The chapters in Part I of this book speak especially clearly to the ways in which we see infants as competent and innately motivated to learn (Principle 3) within their everyday social encounters with caring, responsive adults and peers. Through playful interactions (Chapter 2), peer friendships (Chapter 3), and an active engagement with humor through the everyday routines of childcare (Chapter 4), infants and toddlers experience a socially integrated curriculum that strengthens their unique sense of self and nurtures both individual and group learning and development (Principle 4).

To support infants' holistic way of learning, teachers must be prepared to engage in an intellectually informed teaching practice that synthesizes both caring for and educating infants and toddlers in group care settings. This way of teaching emphasizes the social and physical environments of learning, not simply the skills and content associated with later schooling (Loizou & Recchia, 2018; Peterson & Wittmer, 2013). Infant–toddler curriculum and pedagogy must be integrated into the daily lives of infants and toddlers and across developmental domains.

Respecting what babies know and can learn, as well as their individual ways of learning, is foundational to responsive pedagogy with infants and toddlers (Hammond, 2009; Petrie & Owen, 2005). Through this respectful approach to infants' and toddlers' ways of being and sense of time (Principle 5), caregivers demonstrate their trust in children's ability to be active agents in their own care and learning. As described in Chapters 5 and 6, teachers' and caregivers' ways of understanding and being with infants and toddlers can have a powerful impact on their learning experiences (Institute of Medicine and National Research Council, 2015). When caregivers' ways of responding do not recognize children's competence, opportunities to nurture their growth and learning in the moment and to strengthen trust in the relationship may be lost, creating future gaps in understanding and connectedness (National Scientific Council on the Developing Child, 2007).

As we learn further about what happens in group care settings, we see more clearly the active role that infants and toddlers play in constructing friendships and peer culture, often demonstrated through their playful and humorous interactions. Their ability to form complex social networks within their families, with their caregivers, and with their peers in childcare inform teaching practices in early care and education. As caregivers become aware of infants' growing competencies and learn to better support them, they must also rethink their own roles in infant and toddler play, taking care not to undermine children's agency through overdirecting playful encounters or imposing their own ideas without being open to children's offers (Singer, 2016).

INFANTS' AND TODDLERS' RIGHTS TO RESPONSIVE AND LOVING CARE

For an increasing number of infants and toddlers, childcare is likely to be the first place for negotiating separation from their families. Relationship-based childcare can offer the opportunity for children to experience feelings of belonging and community (Seland et al., 2015), beyond their familiar family context. Recchia and Fincham (2019) embed this sense of community within a human rights perspective, suggesting that childcare centers offer infants and toddlers their initial experiences as citizens within a new shared community. How a childcare community supports its young citizens' rights to responsive and loving care will be influenced by many contextual factors, including routines, schedules, and use of time and space. When centers are governed by adult schedules and needs that require both teachers and children to conform to rigid rules and expectations, it may be difficult for teachers to prioritize responsive and loving care and to honor infants' and toddlers' rights (Te One, 2011) and promote their well-being.

Despite the evidence reported throughout this book and in the literature about the significance of nurturing relationships in early care and education for infants and toddlers, the field of infant childcare is currently facing many challenges in meeting the relationship needs of infants, toddlers, and families (Lally, 2013). Although increasing numbers of children from birth to 3 years are being cared for by nonparental caregivers (Horm et al., 2013), quality of care varies widely, and policies guiding practice are inconsistent across states and countries (Hyson & Tomlinson, 2014). Infant–toddler teachers continue to be the most poorly paid in the field, and the least regulated regarding certification and professional preparation. Staff turnover remains high, and many early childhood teachers have not been prepared with specific knowledge about this age group, including specialized approaches to teaching infants and understanding their holistic and integrated ways of learning (Gloeckler & La Paro, 2016).

We believe that all infants and toddlers in childcare deserve to be cared for within professional and loving relationships, which should be prioritized throughout the caregiving system (Principle 1). Partnering with families, who are the primary caregivers and educators of their children (Principle 2), childcare teachers are positioned to engage in nurturing relationships that provide infants and toddlers a sense of belonging and support their connections with others within a larger social network. These early emotional relationships can also act as a buffer to current environmental stress and provide a powerful foundation for negotiating future stress (Degotardi & Pearson, 2014).

As described in Chapter 5, relationship-based teaching and learning and responsive and loving care require a special type of dialogue and reciprocity between infants and their teachers. Developing these deeper understandings of and ways of being with each other in the everyday moments of childcare will happen in different ways with diverse adults and children in various childcare contexts (Degotardi & Pearson, 2014). However, as noted throughout earlier chapters, we believe some essential components should undergird early care and education for infants and toddlers across settings and particular program constraints. These include respecting the youngest children as worthy of loving care; ensuring the caregiving environment is physically and psychologically safe; providing infants the freedom to make choices in their play and to be themselves; giving them space to explore and interact with peers; and ensuring that at least one caring adult has made a meaningful connection with each child.

The social-emotional learning that happens naturally for babies is embedded in their early interactions with others. Infants and toddlers respond to the physical and dispositional ways that their caregivers react to them and to others in the care setting, including other children and adults. They learn to adjust their ways of expressing themselves in line with the emotional behaviors they observe, and the ways those behaviors make them feel, even when those behaviors are directed to others in the environment (Meltzoff & Kuhl, 2016). When childcare teachers mindfully and respectfully observe and support children's initiations, they create a shared intersubjective space within which children feel free to express themselves, allowing them to be agentic participants in shaping the curriculum (Seland et al., 2015). By providing an encouraging and responsive presence, teachers support infants' and toddlers' natural competence and motivation to learn (Principle 3) (Peterson & Wittmer, 2013).

Taking this one step further, when teachers take a non-intrusive stance that supports children's initiations in play rather than expecting children to respond to their teacher-led ideas or a standard curriculum, they encourage children to define, follow, and elaborate on their own interests and ways of seeing and being in the world. Instead of hurrying children toward the next activity or milestone, respecting infants' and toddlers' own sense of time allows them to be in their own process of being who they are and becoming who they will be, creating time and space for new learning to emerge (Mozere, 2007).

INFANT-TODDLER CARE AS A "HOME" FOR FOSTERING COMMUNITY AND SUBJECTIVE WELL-BEING

What happens in the everyday relationship world of infants, toddlers, families, teachers, and administrators within "shared intersubjective spaces" (Seland et al., 2015) is at the center of and perhaps the most significant indicator of quality infant–toddler care (Dalli et al., 2011). Fostering a sense of community (Principle 6) in an infant or toddler room begins when teachers practice the art of honoring individual differences in young children as they consider ways to invite all learners as full participants in the group. In recognizing each child's ability "to contribute to decisions made about their care and education" (McMullen et al., 2016, p. 259), infant–toddler teachers make space for children's unique ideas and interests as an integral part of their curriculum and pedagogy. Through social interactions and child-initiated rituals, very young children learn how to connect with their peers, make friends, and come to understand "the rules and skills needed to maintain relationships" within the context of their specific peer culture (Whaley & Rubenstein, 2004, p. 384). Teachers' support and guidance of children's behavior becomes a natural part of building classroom community, helping children to become increasingly aware of themselves and their impact on others (Petrie & Owen, 2005). Alongside their peers and teachers, infants and toddlers come to understand the community culture within their childcare environments, where different children may have different needs, but everyone's needs are important to consider.

These ways of thinking about a center's culture and honoring diversity are also at the heart of working with families as valued community members. Recchia and Fincham (2019) name three areas of emphasis in nurturing community engagement with families: communication, family-centeredness, and cross-cultural caregiving partnerships. Communication is an essential element in building collaborative relationships with families. Ongoing and daily written and/or spoken communication with families conveys a powerful message that they are important members of the caregiving team. An established framework for communication with families provides a vehicle for sharing observations and information that helps build a partnership in caring for their children. When daily connections with families are an integral part of center practice, a bond is established that can make it easier to engage in discussions when issues or disagreements about expectations and practices arise. As described in Chapter 7, connecting and communicating with families through a lens that honors and prioritizes relationships throughout the caregiving system (Principle 1), and respects families as the primary caregivers and educators of their children (Principle 2), invites collaborative care and supports family and caregiver well-being.

Looking through a lens of family-centeredness within a caring community asks administrators and caregivers to "integrate attention to parents at all points of connection" (Cole & Lerner, 2015, p. 3). As family involvement is prioritized at the center, parents are supported to feel welcome, understood, and respected. Building cross-cultural partnerships with families can be challenging for all members of the community and relies on a spirit of cooperation. Finding ways to understand and appreciate contradictions in diverse ways of knowing may be a starting point for crossing boundaries and working with families to support their cultural values without compromising practitioners' professional knowledge and expertise (Barrera & Corso, 2003).

CONCLUDING THOUGHTS

In this chapter we have summarized key elements described throughout the book that support quality infant and toddler childcare through authentic and responsive relationship-based practice. We hope you will consider the ways that these components of care can be embedded in a variety of childcare settings to address the needs of diverse children, families, and teachers. Infant and toddler childcare that reflects these conceptual ideas can enhance the lives of all members of the community and complement the roles that families play in their children's lives. In bringing these ideas together, we have emphasized the critical importance of specialized professional preparation to understand and work with this age group. For those who are or aspire to be infant–toddler practitioners, we hope these ideas find their way into your practice.

References

Ailwood, J. (2008). Mothers, teachers, maternalism and early childhood education and care: Some historical connections. *Contemporary Issues in Early Childhood, 8*(2), 157–165.

Andrews, M. (2012). *Exploring play for early childhood studies.* Sage/Learning Matters.

Ashby, N., & Neilsen-Hewett, C. (2012). Approaches to conflict and conflict resolution in toddler relationships. *Journal of Early Childhood Research, 10*(2), 145–161. https://doi.org/10.1177/1476718X11430070

Aslanian, T. K. (2015). Getting behind discourses of love, care and maternalism in early childhood education. *Contemporary Issues in Early Childhood, 16*(2), 153–165.

Axtmann, A., & Detweiler, A. (2005). *The visit: Observation, reflection, synthesis for training and relationship building.* Paul H. Brookes Publishing Company.

Banerjee, R., & Luckner, J. (2014). Training needs of early childhood professionals who work with children and families who are culturally and linguistically diverse. *Infants and Young Children, 27,* 43–59.

Barned, N. E., Knapp, N. F., & Neuharth-Pritchett, N. (2011). Knowledge and attitudes of early childhood preservice teachers regarding the inclusion of children with autism spectrum disorder. *Journal of Early Childhood Teacher Education, 32*(4), 302–321.

Barrera, I., & Corso, R. M. (2002). Cultural competency as skilled dialogue. *Topics in Early Childhood Special Education, 22,* 103–113.

Barrera, I., & Corso, R. (2003). *Skilled dialogue: Strategies for responding to cultural diversity in early childhood.* Paul H. Brookes Publishing.

Beck, L. M. (2013). Fieldwork with infants: What preservice teachers can learn from taking care of babies. *Journal of Early Childhood Teacher Education, 34*(1), 7–22.

Bergen, D. (2019). Young children's play and humor development: A close theoretical partnerships. In E. Loizou & S. L., Recchia (Eds.), *Research on young children's humor: Theoretical and practical implications for early childhood education* (pp. 11–28). Springer International Publishing.

Bergen, D., Lee, L., DiCarlo, C., & Burnett, G. (2020). *Enhancing brain development in infants and young children: Strategies for caregivers and educators.* Teachers College Press.

Bergen, D., Reid, R., & Torelli, L. (2009). *Educating and caring for very young children: The infant/toddler curriculum* (2nd ed.). Teachers College Press.

Bhavnagri, N. P., & Gonzalez-Mena, J. (1997). The cultural context of infant caregiving. *Childhood Education, 74,* 2–8.

Bradley, R. H., & Vandell, D. L. (2007). Child care and the well-being of children. *Archives of Pediatric and Adolescent Medicine, 161,* 669–676.

Brenner, J., & Mueller, E. (1982). Shared meaning in boy toddlers' peer relations. *Child Development, 53,* 380–391.

Brock, A., & Jarvis, P. (2019). Born to play. Babies and toddlers playing. In A. Brock, P. Jarvis, & Y. Olusoga (Eds.), *Perspectives on play. Learning for life* (3rd ed.) (pp. 119–144). Routledge.

Brownell, C., & Brown, E. (1992). Peers and play in infants and toddlers. In V. Van Hasselt & M. Hersen (Eds.), *Handbook of social development* (pp. 183–200). Plenum.

Brownell, C. A., & Kopp, C. B. (Eds.). (2007). *Socioemotional development in the toddler years: Transitions and transformations.* The Guilford Press.

Brownell, C., Ramani, G., & Zerwas, S. (2006). Becoming a social partner with peers: Cooperation and social understanding in one-and two-year-olds. *Child Development, 77,* 803–821. https://doi.org/10.1111/j.1467-8624.2006.t01-1-.x-i1

Bruce, T. (2017). In T. Bruce, P. Hakkarainen, & M. Bredikyte (Eds.), *Routledge international handbook of early childhood play* (pp. 9–21). Routledge-Taylor & Francis Group.

Bukowski, W. M., & Hoza, B. (1989). Popularity and friendship: Issues in theory, measurement, and outcome. In T. J. Berndt & G. W. Ladd (Eds.), *Peer relationships in child development* (pp. 15–45). John Wiley & Sons.

Bussey, C., & Hill, D. (2017). Care as curriculum: Investigating teachers' views on the learning in care. *Early Child Development and Care, 187*(1), 128–137. https://doi.org/10.1080/03004430.2016.1152963

Caplan, M., Vespo, J., Pedersen, J., & Hay, D. F. (1991). Conflict and its resolution in small groups of one and two year olds. *Child Development, 62*(1), 1513–1524. https://doi.org/10.1111/j.1467-8624.1991.tb01622.x

Chen, D. W., Fein, G. G., Killen, M., & Tam, H. (2001). Peer conflicts of preschool children: Issues, resolution, incidence, and age-related patterns. *Early Education and Development, 12*(4), 523–544. https://doi.org/10.1207/s15566935eed1204_3

Cochran-Smith, M., & Lytle, S. L. (1999). Relationships of knowledge and practice: Teacher learning in communities. *Review of Research in Education, 24,* 249–305.

Cole, P. A., & Lerner, C. (2015). Zero to Three *comments on family engagement before the interagency policy board.* www.zerotothree.org/resource/zero-to -three-comments-on-family-engagement

Colley, H. (2006). Learning to labor with feeling: Class, gender and emotion in childcare education and training. *Contemporary Issues in Early Childhood, 7*(1), 15.

Corsaro, W. (1985). *Friendship and peer culture in the early years.* Ablex Publishing Corporation.

Cousins, S. B. (2017). Practitioners' constructions of love in early childhood education and care. *International Journal of Early Years Education, 25*(1), 16–29.

Cranton, P. (2006). *Understanding and promoting transformative learning: A guide for educators of adults* (2nd ed.). Jossey-Bass.

Croft, C. (2010). Talking to families of infants and toddlers about developmental delays. *Young Children, 65,* 44–46.

References

Dalli, C. (1999). Starting childcare before three: Narratives of experience from a tri-partite focus (Unpublished doctoral dissertation). Victoria University of Wellington.

Dalli, C. (2006). Re-visioning love and care in early childhood: Constructing the future of our profession. *The First Years. Nga Tau Tuatahi. New Zealand Journal of Infant and Toddler Education, 8*(1), 5–11.

Dalli, C. (2008). Pedagogy, knowledge and collaboration: Toward a ground-up perspective on professionalism. *European Early Childhood Education Research Journal, 16*(2), 171–185. https://doi.org/10.1080/13502930802141600

Dalli, C., White, E. J., Rockel, J., & Duhn, I. (2011). Quality early childhood education for under-two-year-olds: What should it look like? A literature review. Ministry of Education, New Zealand.

Darling-Hammond, L. (2006). Constructing 21st century teacher education. *Journal of Teacher Education, 57*(3), 300–314.

Davidov, M., Zahn-Waxler, C., Roth-Hanania, R., & Knafo, A. (2013). Concern for others in the first year of life: Theory, evidence, and avenues for research. *Child Development Perspectives, 7*(2), 126–131. https://doi.org/10.1111/cdep.12028

Davis, B., & Degotardi, S. (2015). Educators' understandings of, and support for, infant peer relationships in early childhood settings. *Journal of Early Childhood Research, 13*(1), 64–78. https://doi.org/10.1177/1476718X14538600

Davis, B., & Dunn, R. (2018). Making the personal visible: Emotion in the nursery. *Early Child Development and Care, 188*(7), 905–923. https://doi.org/10.080/030044320.2018.1439487

Degotardi, S. (2010). High-quality interactions with infants: Relationships with early-childhood practitioners' interpretations and qualification levels in play and routine contexts. *International Journal of Early Years Education, 18*(1), 27–41. https://doi.org/10.1080/09669761003661253

Degotardi, S. (2017). Joint attention in infant–toddler early childhood programs: Its dynamics and potential for collaborative learning. *Contemporary Issues in Early Childhood, 18*(4), 409–421. https://doi.org/10.1177/1463949117742786

Degotardi, S., Page, J., & White, E. J. (2017). (Re)conceptualising relationships in infant–toddler pedagogy. *Contemporary Issues in Early Childhood, 18*(4), 355–361. doi:10.1177/1463949117742760

Degotardi, S., & Pearson, E. (2009). Relationship theory in the nursery: Attachment and beyond. *Contemporary Issues in Early Childhood, 10*(2), 144–155. https://doi.org/10.2304/ciec.2009.10.2.144

Degotardi, S., & Pearson, E. (2014). *The Relationship worlds of infants and toddlers: Multiple perspectives from early years theory and practice.* Open University.

Derman-Sparks, L., & Edwards, J. O. (2010). *Anti-bias education for young children and ourselves.* National Association for the Education of Young Children.

Dewey, J. (1998/1933). What is thinking? In *How We Think* (pp. 3–16). Houghton Mifflin Company.

Dunham, P., & Moore, C. (1995). Current themes in research on joint attention. In C. Moore & P. J. Dunham (Eds.), *Joint Attention: Its Origins and Role in Development* (pp. 15–28). Erlbaum.

Dunn, J. (2004). *Children's friendships: The beginnings of intimacy*. Blackwell Publishing.

Eckerman, C. O., Davis, C. C., & Didow, S. M. (1989). Toddlers' emerging ways of achieving social coordinations with a peer. *Child Development, 60*, 440–453. https://doi.org/10.2307/1130988

Eckerman, C. O., & Peterman, K. (2001). Peers and infant social/communicative development. In G. Bremner & A. Fogel (Eds.), *Blackwell handbook of infant development* (pp. 326–350). Blackwell Publishers.

Eckerman, C. O., Whatley, J., & Kutz, S. (1975). Growth of social play with peers during the second year of life. *Developmental Psychology, 11*, 42–49.

Elfer, P. (2012). Emotion in nursery work: Work discussion as a model of critical professional reflection. *Early Years: Journal of International Research and Development, 32*(2), 129–141.

Elfer, P. (2015). Emotional aspects of nursery policy and practice, progress and prospect. *European Early Childhood Education Research Journal, 23*(4), 497–511.

Elfer, P., & Dearnley, D. (2007). Nurseries and emotional well-being: Evaluating an emotionally containing model of professional development. *Early Years: An International Journal of Research and Development, 27*(3), 267–279. https://doi.org/10.1080/09575140701594418

Elfer, P., Goldschmied, E., & Selleck, D. (2003). *Key persons in the nursery: Building relationships for quality provision*. David Fulton Publishing.

Elfer, P., & Page, J. (2015). Pedagogy with babies: Perspectives of eight nursery managers. *Early Child Development and Care, 185*(11–12), 1762–1782. https://doi.org/10.1080/03004430.2015.1028399

Elicker, J., Ruprecht, K. M., & Anderson, T. (2014). Observing infants' and toddlers' relationships and interactions in group care. In L. J. Harrison & J. Sumsion (Eds.), *Lived spaces of infant–toddler education and care: Exploring diverse perspectives on theory, research, and practice* (pp. 131–145). Springer.

Engdahl, I. (2011). Toddler interaction during play in the Swedish preschool. *Early Child Development and Care, 181*(10), 1421–1439. https://doi.org/10.1080/03004430.2010.533269

Engdahl, I. (2012). Doing friendship during the second year of life in a Swedish preschool. *European Early Childhood Education Research Journal, 20*(1), 83–98. https://doi.org/10.1080/1350293X.2012.650013

Feiman-Nemser, S. (2008). Teacher Learning: How do teachers learn to teach? In M. Cochran-Smith, S. Feiman-Nemser, D. J. McIntyre, & K. E. Demers (Eds.), *Handbook of research on teacher education: Enduring questions in changing contexts* (pp. 697–705). Routledge.

Fogel, A. (2009). *Infancy: Infant, family and society*. Sloan.

Formosinho, J. (2016). Pedagogic documentation. In Oliveira-Formosinho & C. Pascal (Eds.), *Assessment and evaluation for transformation in early childhood* (pp. 107–128). Routledge.

Foss, M. (1995). "Like mud not fireworks." The place of passion in the development of literacy. Paper presented at the symposium teaching as an art, writing as a craft. The English-Language Arts Consortium of the Greater Bay Area, Redwood Shores, California.

References

Gallo-Fox, J., & Scantlebury, K. (2015). "It isn't necessarily sunshine and daisies every time": Coplanning opportunities and challenges when student teaching. *Asia-Pacific Journal of Teacher Education, 43*(4), 324–337. http://dx.doi.org/10.1080/1359866X.2015.1060294

Gallo-Fox, J., & Scantlebury, K. (2016). Coteaching as professional development for cooperating teachers. *Teaching and Teacher Education, 60,* 191–202. http://dx.doi.org/10.1016/j.tate.2016.08.007

Gerhardt, S. (2004). *Why love matters: How affection shapes a baby's brain.* Brunner-Routledge.

Gloeckler, L., & La Paro, K. M. (2016). Toddlers and child care: A time for discussion, dialogue, and change. *Zero to Three, 36*(2), 45–52.

Goldschmied, E., & Jackson, S. (2004). *People under three: Young children in day care.* Routledge.

Goldstein, L. S. (1998). *Teaching with love: A feminist approach to early childhood education.* Peter Lang.

Goldstein, L. S., & Lake, V. E. (2000). "Love, love, and more love for children": Exploring preservice teachers' understandings of caring. *Teaching and Teacher Education, 16*(8), 861–872.

González, N., Moll, L. C., & Amanti, C. (Eds.). (2005). *Funds of knowledge: Theorizing practices in households, communities, and classrooms.* Lawrence Erlbaum.

Gonzalez-Mena, J. (2001). Cross-cultural infant care and issues of equity and social justice. *Contemporary Issues in Early Childhood, 2*(3), 368–371. https://doi.org/10.2304/ciec.2001.2.3.8

Gonzalez-Mena, J., & Bhavnagri, N. P. (2000). Diversity and infant/toddler caregiving, *Young Children, 55*(5), 31–35. http://www.jstor.org/stable/42727845

Gonzalez-Mena, J., & Eyer, D. W. (2007). *Infants, toddlers, and caregivers: A curriculum of respectful, responsive care and education* (7th ed.). McGraw-Hill.

Gonzales-Mena, J. & Eyer, D. W. (2012). *Infants, toddlers, and caregivers: A curriculum of respectful, responsive, relationship-based care and education.* (9th ed.) McGraw-Hill.

Goodfellow, J. (2014). Infants initiating encounters with peers in group care environments. In L. J. Harrison & J. Sumsion (Eds.), *Lived spaces of infant–toddler education and care: Exploring diverse perspectives on theory, research, practice and policy* (pp. 201–210). Springer.

Goodnough, K., Osmond-Johnson, P., Dibbon, D., Glassman, M., & Stevens, K. (2009). Exploring a triad model of student teaching: Pre-service teacher and cooperating teacher perceptions. *Teaching and Teacher Education, 25*(2), 285–296.

Goouch, K., & Powell, S. (2013). *The baby room: Principles, policy and practice.* Open University Press.

Gopnik, A. (2010). *The philosophical baby: What children's minds tell us about truth, love, and the meaning of life.* Farrar, Straus & Giroux.

Gordon Biddle, K. A., Garcia-Nevarez, A., Roundtree Henderson, W. J., & Valero-Kerrick, A. (2014). *Early childhood education: Becoming a professional.* Sage.

Greve, A. (2009). Friendship and participation among young children in a Norwegian kindergarten. In D. Berthelsen, J. Brownlee, & E. Johansson (Eds.),

Participatory learning in the early years, research and pedagogy (pp. 78–92). Oxon/Routledge.

Grossman, S. (2008). "I just don't like that kid." Confronting and managing personal feelings about children. *Childhood Education, 84*(3), 147–149.

Gupta, A. (2006). Early experiences and personal funds of knowledge and beliefs of immigrant and minority teacher candidates dialog with theories of child development in a teacher education classroom. *Journal of Early Childhood Teacher Education, 27*(1), 3–18.

Hammond, R. A. (2009). *Respecting babies: A guide to Educaring® for parents & professionals* (2nd ed.). Zero to Three.

Hartup, W. W. (1996). Cooperation, close relationships, and cognitive development. In W. M. Bukowski, A. F. Newcomb, & W. W. Hartup (Eds.), *The company they keep: Friendship in childhood and adolescence* (pp. 213–237). Cambridge University Press.

Hartup, W. W., Laursen, B., Stewart, M. I., & Eastenson, A. (1988). Conflict and the friendship relations of young children. *Child Development, 59*(6), 1590–1600. https://doi.org/10.2307/1130673

Hay, D. (1984). Social conflict in early childhood. In G. Whitehurst (Ed.), *Annals of child development* (Vol. 1. pp. 1–44). JAI.

Hay, D. F., Nash, A., & Pederson, J. (1983). Interaction between six-month-old peers. *Child Development, 54*(3), 557–562. https://doi.org/10.2307/1130042

Hay, D., & Ross, H. (1982). The social nature of early conflict. *Child Development, 53*, 105–113. https://doi.org/10.2307/1129642

Hochschild, A. R. (1983). *The managed heart: Commercialization of human feeling.* University of California Press.

Hoicka, E., & Akhtar, N. (2012). Early humour production. *British Journal of Developmental Psychology, 30*, 586–603. https://doi.org/10.1111/j.2044-835X .2011.02075.x

Hoicka E., & Gattis, M. (2012). Acoustic differences between humorous and sincere communicative intentions. *British Journal of Developmental Psychology, 30*(4), 531–549. https://doi.org/10.1111/j.2044-835X.2011.02062.x

Hoicka, E., & Martin, C. (2016). Two-year-olds distinguish pretending and joking. *Child Development, 87*(3), 916–928. https://doi.org/10.1111/cdev.12526

Honig, A. S. (1993). Mental health for babies: What do theory and research teach us? *Young Children, 48*(3), 69–76.

Horm, D. M., Hyson, M. & Winton, P. J. (2013). Research on early childhood teacher education: Evidence from three domains and recommendations for moving forward. *Journal of Early Childhood Teacher Education, (34)*1, 95–112.

Howes, C. (1983). Patterns of friendship. *Child Development, 54*, 1041–1053.

Howes, C. (1985). Sharing fantasy: Social pretend play in toddlers. *Child Development, 56*, 1253–1258.

Howes, C. (1988). Peer interaction of young children. *Monographs of the Society for Research in Child Development, 48*(217), 1–88.

Howes, C. (1996). The earliest friendships. In W. M. Bukowski, A. F. Newcomb, & W. W. Hartup (Eds.), *The company they keep: Friendship in childhood and adolescence* (pp. 66–86). Cambridge University Press.

Howes, C., & Hamilton, C. E. (1992). Children's relationships with caregivers: Mothers and child care teachers. *Child Development, 63*, 859–878.

References

Howes, C., & Hamilton, C. E. (1993). The changing experience of child care: Changes in teachers and in teacher–child relationships and children's social competence with peers. *Early Childhood Research Quarterly, 8*, 15–32.

Howes, C., Matheson, C. C., & Hamilton, C. E. (1994). Maternal, teacher, and child care history correlates of children's relationships with peers. *Child Development, 65(1)*, 264–273. https://doi.org/10.2307/1131380

Howes, C., & Ritchie, S. (2002). *A matter of trust: Connecting teachers and learners in the early childhood classroom.* Teachers College Press.

Hughes, A. M. (2010). *Developing play for the under 3s—treasure basket and heuristic play* (2nd ed.). Routledge.

Hughes, B. (2001). *Evolutionary playwork and reflective analytic practice* (2nd ed.). Routledge.

Hyson, M., & Tomlinson, H. B. (2014). *The early years matter: Education, care, and the well-being of children, Birth–8.* Teachers College Press.

Institute of Medicine and National Research Council (2015). *Transforming the workforce for children birth through age 8: A unifying foundation.* The National Academies Press.

Jacobson, T. (2018). When teachers face themselves: Managing our emotions when children seek attention. *Exchange* (September/October) 35–37.

Jung, J., & Recchia, S. (2013). Scaffolding infants' play through empowering and individualizing teaching practices. *Early Education & Development, 24(6)*, 829–850. https://doi.org/10.1080/10409289.2013.744683

Jung, J., Recchia, S. L., & Ottley, J. (2021). Transitioning from primary-grade classrooms to infant/toddler rooms: Early childhood preservice teachers' growth and challenges. *Journal of Early Childhood Teacher Education, 42(3)*, 245–264. https://doi.org/10.1080/10901027.2020.1735585

Kemple, K. M. (1991). Research in review: Preschool children's peer acceptance and social interaction. *Young Children, 46(5)*, 47–54.

Lally, J. R. (1995). The impact of childcare policies on infant/toddler identity formation. *Young Children, 51(1)*, 58–67.

Lally, J. R. (2009). The science and psychology of infant–toddler care: How an understanding of early learning has transformed childcare. *Zero to Three, 29(2)*, 47–53.

Lally, J. R. (2013). *For our babies: Ending the invisible neglect of America's infants.* Teachers College Press.

Lally, J. R., Mangione, P., & Singer, S. (2002, November). *The importance of intimacy in infant toddler care: Looking at how the combination of small groups, primary caregiver assignment, and continuity benefit the developing child.* Paper presented at the Annual Conference of the National Association for the Education of Young Children, New York, New York.

Lally, J. R., Torres, Y. L., & Phelps, P. C. (2010, February 8). *How to care for infants and toddlers in groups.* Zero to Three Parenting Resource. www.zerotothree.org/resources/77-how-to-care-for-infants-and-toddlers-in-groups

Lee, S. Y. (2006). A journey to a close, secure, and synchronous relationship: Infant–caregiver *relationship* development in a childcare context. *Journal of Early Childhood Research, 4(2)*, 133–151. https://doi.org/10.1177/1476718X06063533

Lee, S. Y., Shin, M., & Recchia, S. L. (2016). Primary caregiving as a framework for preparing early childhood pre-service students to understand and work with infants. *Early Education and Development, 27*(3), 336–351. https://doi.org/10.1080/10409289.2015.1076675

Lewis, M., Young, G., Brooks, J., & Michalson, L. (1975). The beginning of friendship. In M. Lewis & L. A. Rosenblum (Eds.), *Friendship and peer relations* (pp. 27–66). John Wiley & Sons,

Licht, B., Simoni, H., & Perrig-Chiello, P. (2008). Conflict between peers in infancy and toddler age: What do they fight about? *Early Years, 28*(3), 235–249. https://doi.org/10.1080/09575140802065458

Lillemyr, O. F. (2009). *Taking play seriously. Children and play in early childhood education—an exciting challenge.* Information Age Publishing.

Lindahl, M., & Pramling Samuelsson, I. (2002). Imitation and variation: Reflections on toddlers' strategies for learning. *Scandinavian Journal of Educational Research, 46*(1), 25–45.

Loizou, E. (2004a). Funny babies: Humor and power in infancy. *Zero to Three, 24*(1), 17–21.

Loizou, E. (2004b). Humorous bodies and humorous minds: Humor within the social context of an infant child care setting. *European Early Childhood Education Research Journal, 12*(1), 15–28.

Loizou, E. (2005a). Infant humor: The theory of the absurd and the empowerment theory. *International Journal of Early Years Education, 13*(1), 43–53.

Loizou, E. (2005b). Humor: A different kind of play. *European Early Childhood Education Research Journal, 13*(2), 97–109.

Loizou, E. (2007). Humor as a means of regulating one's social self: Two infants with unique humorous personas. *Early Child Development and Care, 177*(2), 195–205.

Loizou, E. (2017). Children's socio-dramatic play typologies and teacher play involvement within the breadth of the zone of proximal development. In T. Bruce, P. Hakkarainen, & M. Bredikyte (Eds.), *Routledge international handbook of early childhood play* (pp. 151–166). Routledge-Taylor & Francis Group.

Loizou, E. (2019). *Constructive play: Children's play skills and teacher's involvement.* Early Childhood Research Lab. Online. doi:10.13140/RG.2.2.33863.44960

Loizou, E. (2021). *Small blocks and building materials.* In D. Bergen (Ed.), *The ultimate handbook of developmentally appropriate toys* (pp. 49–60). Rowman & Littlefield

Loizou, E., & Demetriou, M. (2019). Infancy pedagogy and praxis. *European Early Childhood Education Research Journal, 27*(4), 436–453.

Loizou, E., & Recchia, S. L. (2018). In-service infant teachers re-envision their practice through a professional development program. *Early Education and Development, 29*(1), 91–103. doi:10.1080/10409289.2017.1343561

Loizou, E., & Recchia, S. L. (Eds.). (2019). *Research on young children's humor: Theoretical and practical implications for early childhood education.* Springer International Publishing

Løkken, G. (2000). The playful quality of toddling style. *International Journal of Qualitative Studies in Education, 13*(5), 531–42.

Løkken, G. (2009). The construction of "toddler" in early childhood pedagogy. *Contemporary Issues in Early Childhood, 10*(1), 35–42. https://doi.org/10.2304/ciec.2009.10.1.35

References

Manning-Morton, J. (2006). The personal is professional: Professionalism and the birth to three practitioner. *Contemporary Issues in Early Childhood, 7*(1), 42–52. https://doi.org/10.2304/ciec.2006.7.1.42

Markus, H. R., & Kitayama, S. (1991). Culture and the self: Implications for cognition, emotion, and motivation. *Psychological Review, 98*(2), 224–253. https://doi.org/10.1037/0033-295X.98.2.224

McDevitt, S. E., & Recchia, S. L. (2022). How toddlers new to childcare become members of a classroom community. *Early Child Development and Care, 192*(3), 481–498. https://doi.org/10.1080/03004430.2020.1767607

McGaha, C. G., Cummings, R., Lippard, B., & Dallas, K. (2011). Relationship building: Infants, toddlers, and 2-year-olds. *ECRP: Early Childhood Research and Practice, 13*(1). http://ecrp.uiuc.edu/ v13n1/mcgaha.html

McGhee, P. E. (1979). *Humor: Its origin and development.* W. H. Freeman.

McGhee, P. (2010). *Humor: The lighter path to resilience and health.* Author.

McGhee, P. (2019). Humor in the ECE classroom: A neglected form of play whose time has come. In E. Loizou & S. L., Recchia (Eds.), *Research on young children's humor: Theoretical and practical implications for early childhood education* (pp. 83–106). Springer International Publishing.

McMullen, M. B., & Apple, P. (2012). Babies [and their families] on board! Directors juggle the key elements of infant/toddler care and education. *Young Children, 67,* 42–48.

McMullen, M. B., Buzzelli, C., & Yun, N. (2016). Pedagogies of care for wellbeing. In T. David, S. Powell, & K. Goouch (Eds.), *Routledge Handbook of Philosophies and Theories of Early Childhood Education* (pp. 259–268). Routledge.

McMullen, M. B., & McCormick, K. (2016). Flourishing in transactional care systems: Caring with infant and toddler caregivers about well-being. In D. Narvaez, J. M. Braungart-Reiker, L. E. Miller-Graff, L. T. Gettler, & P. D. Hastings (Eds.), *Contexts for young child flourishing: Evolution, family, and society* (pp. 267–287). Oxford University Press.

Meltzoff, A. N. (2010). Social cognition and the origins of imitation, empathy, and theory of mind. In U. Goswami (Ed.), *The Wiley Blackwell handbook of childhood cognitive development* (2nd ed.) (pp. 49–75). Wiley-Blackwell.

Meltzoff, A. N., & Kuhl, P. K. (2016). Exploring the infant social brain: What's going on in there? *Zero to Three, 36*(3), 2–9.

Mezirow, J. (1997). Transformative learning: Theory to practice. *New Directions for Adult and Continuing Education, 74,* 5–12.

Miller, K. (2000). Caring for the little ones: Friendships in the baby room. *Child Care Information Exchange, 133,* 62–66.

Miller, P., Votruba-Drzal, E., Coley, R. L., & Koury, A. S. (2014). Immigrant families' use of early childcare: Predictors of care type. *Early Childhood Research Quarterly, 29,* 484–498.

Mireault, G. C., & Reddy, V. (2016). *Humor in infants: Developmental and psychological perspectives.* Springer Science + Business Media. https://doi.org/10.1007/978-3-319-38963-9

Morrissey, A. M. (2014). Scaffolding, analysis and materials: Contributing factors in an unexpected finding of advanced infant/toddler pretend play? *Journal of Early Childhood Research, 12*(2), 195–213.

Movahedazarhouligh, S. (2018). Teaching play skills to children with disabilities: Research-based interventions and practices. *Early Childhood Education Journal, 46,* 587–599.

Mozere, L. (2007). In early childhood: What's language about? *Educational Philosophy and Theory, 39*(3), 291–299.

Mueller, E., & Lucas, T. (1975). A developmental analysis of peer interaction among toddlers. In M. Lewis & L. A. Rosenblum (Eds.), *Friendship and peer relations* (pp. 223–258). John Wiley & Sons.

Mueller, E., & Vandell, D. (1979). Infant–Infant interaction. In J. D. Osofsky (Ed.), *Handbook of infant development* (pp. 591–622). John Wiley & Sons.

Muir, E. (1992). Watching, waiting, and wondering: Applying psychoanalytic principles to mother–infant intervention. *Infant Mental Health Journal, 13*(4), 319–328.

Mundy, P., & Newell, L. (2007). Attention, joint attention, and social cognition. *Current Directions in Psychological Science, 16*(5), 269–274. https://doi.org/10.1111/j.1467-8721.2007.00518.x

Murphy, C., & Martin, S. N. (2015). Coteaching in teacher education: Research and practice. *Asia-Pacific Journal of Teacher Education, 43*(4), 277–280. http://dx.doi.org/10.1080/1359866X.2015.1060927

Murphey, D., Cooper, M., & Forrey, N. (2013). *The youngest Americans: A statistical portrait of infants and toddlers in the United States.* Child Trends.

Murray, C. G. (2022). Professional love: The heart of our work. *Exchange, 263,* 34–37.

Musatti, T., Mayer, S., & Pettenati, P. (2017). Toddlers' participation in joint activities with peers in nido. In E. J. White & C. Dalli (Eds.), *Under-three year olds in policy and practice* (pp. 73–86.) Springer.

National Institute of Child Health and Human Development Early Child Care Research Network. (1996). Characteristics of infant child care: Factors contributing to positive caregiving. *Early Childhood Research Quarterly, 11,* 269–306. https://doi.org/10.1016/S0885-2006(96)90009-5

NICHD Early Child Care Research Network. (2001). Child care and children's peer interaction at 24 and 36 months: The NICHD study of early child care. *Child Development, 72*(5), 1478–1500.

National Scientific Council on the Developing Child (2007). *The timing and quality of early experiences combine to shape brain architecture: Working paper No. 5.* www.developingchild.harvard.edu

Nemeth, K. N., & Erdosi, V. (2012). Enhancing practice with infants and toddlers from diverse language and cultural backgrounds. *Young Children, 67*(4), 49–57. http://www.jstor.org/stable/42731220

Nicholson, S., & Reifel, S. (2011). Sink or swim: Child care teachers' perceptions of entry training experiences. *Journal of Early Childhood Teacher Education, 32*(5), 5–25. https://doi.org/10.1080/10901027.2010.547650

Nilsson, P., & Driel, J. (2010). Teaching together and learning together—Primary science student teachers' and their mentors' joint teaching and learning in the primary classroom. *Teaching and Teacher Education, 26,* 1309–1318. http://dx.doi:10.1016/j.tate.2010.03.009

Nimmo, J., & Park, S. (2009). Engaging early childhood teachers in the thinking and practice of inquiry: Collaborative research mentorship as a tool for shifting teacher identity. *Journal of Early Childhood Teacher Education, 30*(2), 93–104.

References

Noddings, N. (2002). *Starting at home: Caring and social policy*. University of California Press.

Norris, D. J. (2010). Raising the educational requirements for teachers in infant toddler classrooms: Implications for institutions of higher education. *Journal of Early Childhood Teacher Education, 31*(2), 146–158. https://doi.org/10.1080/10901021003781221

Osgood, J. (2006). Deconstructing professionalism in early childhood education: Resisting the regulatory gaze. *Contemporary Issues in Early Childhood, 7*(1), 5–14. https://doi.org/10.2304/ciec.2006.7.1.5

Page, J. (2011). Do mothers want professional carers to love their babies? *Journal of Early Childhood Research, 9*(3), 310–323. https://doi.org/10.1177/1476718X114079

Page, J. (2014). Developing professional love in early childhood settings. In L. Harrison & J. Sumsion (Eds.), *Lived spaces of infant–toddler education and care: Exploring diverse perspectives on theory, research and practice* (pp. 119–130). Springer.

Page, J. (2017). Reframing infant–toddler pedagogy through a lens of professional love: Exploring narratives of professional practice in early childhood settings in England. *Contemporary Issues in Early Childhood, 18*(4), 387–399. https://doi.org/10.1177/1463949117742780

Page, J. (2018). Characterizing the principles of professional love in early childhood care and education. *International Journal of Early Years Education, 26*(2), 125–141.

Page, J., Clare, A., & Nutbrown, C. (2013). *Working with babies and children: From birth to three* (2nd ed.). Sage.

Page, J., & Elfer, P. (2013). The emotional complexity of attachment interactions in nursery. *European Early Childhood Education Research Journal, 21*(4), 553–567.

Perino, O., & Besio, S. (2017). Mainstream toys for play. In S. Besio, D. Bulgarelli, & V. Stancheva-Popkostadinova (Eds.), *Play development in children with disabilities* (pp. 181–200). De Gruyter Open Poland.

Peterson, S. H., & Wittmer, D. S. (2013). *Endless opportunities for infant and toddlers curriculum: A relationship-based approach*. Pearson.

Petrie, S., & Owen, S. (Eds.) (2005). *Authentic relationships in group care for infants and toddlers—Resources for infant educarers (RIE) principles into practice*. Jessica Kingsley Publishers.

Piaget, J. (1932/1965). *The moral judgment of the child*. Free Press.

Piper, H., & Smith, H. (2003). "Touch" in educational and child care settings: Dilemmas and responses. *British Educational Research Journal, 29*(6), 879–894.

Puig, V. I., & Recchia, S. L. (2008). The early childhood professional mentoring group: A forum for parallel learning. *Journal of Early Childhood Teacher Education, 29*(4), 340–354. https://doi.org/10.1080/10901020802470168

Purper, C. J., Thai, Y., Frederick, T. V., & Farris, S. (2023). Exploring the challenge of teachers' emotional labor in early childhood settings. *Early Childhood Education Journal, 51*, 781–789. https://doi.org/10.1007/s10643-022-01345-y

Raikes, H. (1993). Relationship duration in infant care: Time with a high-ability teacher and infant-teacher attachment. *Early Childhood Research Quarterly, 8*, 309–325. https://doi.org/10.1016/S0885-2006(05)80070-5

Raikes, H. (1996). A secure base for babies: Applying attachment concepts to the infant care setting. *Young Children, 51*(5), 59–67.

Raikes, H. H., & Edwards, C. P. (2009). *Expanding the dance in infant and toddler caregiving: Enhancing attachment and relationships.* Paul H. Brookes Publishing Co., Inc.

Rausch, A., Joseph, J., Strain, P. S., & Steed, E. A. (2021). Fostering engagement within inclusive settings. *Young Children, 76* (4), 16–21.

Ray, A., Bowman, B., & Robbins, J. (2006). *Preparing early childhood teachers to successfully educate all children: The contribution of four-year undergraduate teacher preparation programs.* Foundation for Child Development.

Recchia, S. L. (2012). Caregiver–child relationships as a context for continuity in childcare. *Early Years: An International Research Journal, 32*(2), 143–157.

Recchia, S. L. (2016). Preparing teachers for infant care and education. In L. J. Couse & S. L. Recchia (Eds.), *Handbook of early childhood teacher education* (pp. 89–103). Routledge.

Recchia, S. L., & Beck, L. (2014). Reflective practice as "enrichment": How new early childhood teachers enact pre-service values in their classrooms. *Journal of Early Childhood Teacher Education,* (3), 203–225.

Recchia, S. L., Beck, L., Esposito, A., & Tarrant, K. (2009). Diverse field experiences as a catalyst for preparing high quality early childhood teachers. *Journal of Early Childhood Teacher Education, 30*(2), 105–122. https://doi.org/10.1080/10901020902885604

Recchia, S. L., & Dvorakova, K. (2012). How three young toddlers transition from an infant to a toddler child care classroom: Exploring the influence of peer relationships, teacher expectations, and changing social contexts. *Early Education and Development, Special Issue: Laboratory Preschools in the 21st Century, 23*(2), 181–201.

Recchia, S. L., & Dvorakova, K. (2018). Moving from an infant to a toddler childcare classroom: Embracing change and respecting individual differences. *Young Children, 73*(3), 43–49.

Recchia, S. L., Fellner, A., & Fincham, E. N. (2022). The rights of the toddler: The complexities of supporting young children's becoming and belonging in an inclusive classroom community. In F. Press & S. Cheeseman (Eds.), *Conceptualizing and reconceptualizing children's rights in infant–toddler early childhood education and care: Transnational conversations.* Springer.

Recchia, S. L., & Fincham, E. N. (2019). The significance of infant–toddler care and education: A call to unite research, policy, and practice. In C. Brown, M. McMullen, and N. File (Eds.), *The Wiley handbook of early childhood care and education* (pp. 197–217). John Wiley & Sons.

Recchia, S. L., & Lee, Y-J. (2004). At the crossroads: Overcoming concerns to envision possibilities for toddlers in inclusive childcare. *Journal of Research in Childhood Education, 19*(2), 175–188. https://doi.org/10.1080/02568540409595063

Recchia, S. L., & Lee, Y-J. (2013). *Inclusion in the early childhood classroom: What makes a difference?* Teachers College Press.

Recchia, S. L., Lee, S. Y., & Shin, M. (2015). Preparing early childhood professionals for relationship-based work with infants. *Journal of Early Childhood Teacher Education, 36*(2), 100–123. https://doi.org/10.1080/10901027.2015.1030523

Recchia, S. L., & Loizou, E. (2002). Becoming an infant caregiver: Three profiles of personal and professional growth. *Journal of Research in Childhood Education, 16*(2), 133–147.

References

Recchia, S. L., & McDevitt, S. (2018). Unraveling universalist perspectives on teaching and caring for infants and toddlers: Finding authenticity in diverse funds of knowledge. *Journal of Research in Childhood Education, 31*(1), 14–31. https://doi.org/10.1080/02568543.2017.1387206

Recchia, S. L., & McDevitt, S. (2023). A place for Miguel: Discovering the power of belonging within an inclusive toddler community. *European Early Childhood Education Research Journal.* https://doi.org/10.1080/1350293X.2022.2159055

Recchia, S. L., & Puig, V. I. (2019). Early childhood teachers finding voice among peers: A reflection on practice. *The New Educator, 15*(1), 51–65. https://doi.org/10.1080/1547688X.2018.1433344

Recchia, S. L., & Shin, M. (2010). "Baby teachers": How pre-service early childhood students transform their conceptions of teaching and learning through an infant practicum. *Early Years, 30*(2), 135–145. https://doi.org/10.1080/09575141003648357

Recchia, S. L., & Shin, M. (2012). In and out of synch: Caregivers' adaptations to infant's developmental changes, *Early Development and Care, 182*(12), 1545–1562. https://doi.org/10.1080/03004430.2011.630075

Recchia, S. L., Shin, M., & Snaider, C. (2018). Where is the love? Developing loving relationships as an essential component of professional infant care. *International Journal of Early Years Education, 26*(2), 142–158. https://doi.org/10.1080/09669760.2018.1461614

Recchia, S. L., & Williams, L. R. (2006). Culture, class, and diversity: Implications for practice. In G. Foley and J. Hochman (Eds.), *Infant mental health in early intervention: Achieving unity in principles and practice* (pp. 267–294). Paul H. Brookes.

Redder, B., & White, J. E. (2017). Implicating teachers in infant-peer relationships: Teacher answerability through alteric acts. *Contemporary Issues in Early Childhood, 18*(4), 422–433. https://doi.org/10.1177/1463949117742782

Reddy, V. (2001). Infant clowns: The interpersonal creation of humour in infancy. *Enfance, 53*(3), 247–256. https://doi.org/10.3917/enf.533. 0247

Reddy, V. (2019). Humor as culture in infancy. In E. Loizou & S. Recchia (Eds.), *Research on young children's humor: Theoretical and practical implications for early childhood education* (pp. 187–201). Springer.

Riley, D., San Juan, R. R., Klinkner, J., & Ramminger, A. (2008). *Social and emotional development: Connecting science and practice in early childhood settings.* National Association for the Education of Young Children.

Rochat, P. (2001). *The infant's world.* Harvard University Press.

Rockel, J. (2009). A pedagogy of care: Moving beyond the margins of managing work and minding babies. *Australian Journal of Early Childhood, 34*(3), 1–8.

Roth, W., & Tobin, K. (2005). Coteaching: from praxis to theory. In W. Roth & K. Tobin (Eds.), *Teaching together, learning together* (pp. 5–26). Peter Lang.

Rutanen, N. (2007). Two-year-old children as co-constructors of culture. *European Early Childhood Education Research Journal, 15*(1), 59–69. https://doi.org/10.1080/13502930601161825

Salamon, A. (2011). How the early years learning framework can help shift pervasive beliefs of the social and emotional capabilities of infants and toddlers. *Contemporary Issues in Early Childhood, 12*(1), 4–10. https://doi.org/10.2304/ciec.2011.12.1.4

Scantlebury, K., Gallo-Fox, J., & Wassell, B. (2008). Coteaching as a model for preservice secondary science teacher education. *Teaching and Teacher Education, 24*(4), 967–981. https://doi.org/10.1016/j.tate.2007.10.008

Seland, M., Sandseter, E. B. H., & Bratterud, Å. (2015). One- to three-year-old children's experience of subjective wellbeing in day care. *Contemporary Issues in Early Childhood, 16*, 70–83.

Sheridan, M. D. (2006). *Play in early childhood. From birth to six years.* Revised and updated by J. Harding & L. Meldon-Smith. Routledge.

Sheridan, M. D. (2009). *From birth to five years.* Revised and updated by A. Shara & H. Cockerill. Routledge.

Shin, M. (2010). Peeking at the relationship world of infant friends and caregivers. *Journal of Early Childhood Research, 9*(1), 1–9. https://doi.org/10.1177/14767 18X10366777

Shin, M. (2012). The role of joint attention in social communication and play among infants. *Journal of Early Childhood Research, 10*(3), 309–317. https://doi.org /10.1177/1476718X12443023

Shin, M. (2015). Enacting caring pedagogy in the infant classroom. *Early Child Development and Care, 185*(3), 496–508. https://doi.org/10.1080/03004430 .2014.940929

Shin, M. (2021a). Exploring multisensory experiences in infants' learning and development. *Early Child Development and Care, 191*(3), 2116–2127. https://doi .org/10.1080/03004430.2019.1695127

Shin, M. (2021b). Love, or not, that's the question: Examining the intersection among love, care, and education. *Contemporary Issues in Early Childhood, 22*(3), 282–285. https://doi.org/10.1177/1463949120902864

Shin, M., & Lee, S. Y. (2011). Exploring the connection between a developmental change and relationship development with caregivers and peers. *Asia-Pacific Journal of Research in Early Childhood Education, 5*(2), 1–26.

Shin, M., & Partyka, T. (2017). Empowering infants through responsive and intentional play activities. *International Journal of Early Years Education, 25*(2), 127–142. https://doi.org/10.1080/09669760.2017.1291331

Shonkoff, J. P. (2010). Building a new biodevelopmental framework to guide the future of early childhood policy. *Child Development, 81*(1), 357–367.

Shonkoff, J. P., & Phillips, D. A. (Eds.) (2000). *From neurons to neighborhoods: The science of early childhood development.* National Academy Press.

Singer, E. (2016). Theories about young children's peer relationships. In T. David, K. Goouch, & S. Powell (Eds.), *The Routledge international handbook of philosophy and theories of early childhood education and care* (pp. 110–118). Routledge.

Singer, E. (2019). Humor, social laughing, and pleasure to function: Three sources of laughter that are intrinsically connected in early childhood. In E. Loizou & S. L. Recchia (Eds.), *Research on young children's humor: Theoretical and practical implications for early childhood education* (pp. 83–106). Springer International Publishing

Singer, E., & de Haan, D. (2007). *The social lives of young children: Play, conflict and moral learning in day care groups.* SWP Publishers.

Slomkowski, C., & Dunn, J. (1996). Young children's understanding of other people's beliefs and feelings and their connected communication with friends. *Developmental Psychology, 32*(3), 442–447. https://doi.org/10.1037/0012-1649.32.3.442

References

Swim, T. J., & Isik-Ercan, Z. (2013). Dispositional development as a form of continuous professional development: Centre-based reflective practices with teachers of (very) young children. *Early Years, 33*(2), 172–185. http://dx.doi.org/10.1080/09575146.2012.753870

Te One, S. (2011). Implementing children's rights in early education. *Australian Journal of Early Childhood, 36*(4), 54–61.

Thompson, R. A. (2016). What more has been learned? The science of early childhood development 15 years after. *Zero to Three, 36*(3), 18–24.

Tomasello, M. (1995). Joint attention as social cognition. In C. Moore & P. J. Dunham (Eds.), *Joint attention: Its origins and role in development* (pp. 103–130). Lawrence Erlbaum.

Tomasello, M. (1999). *The cultural origins of human cognition*. Harvard University Press.

Tortora, S. (2011). The need to be seen: From Winnicott to the mirror neuron system, dance/movement therapy comes of age. *American Journal of Dance Therapy, 33*(1), 4–17. https://doi.org/10.1007/s10465-011-9107-5

Trevarthen, C. (1979). Communication and cooperation in early infancy. A description of primary intersubjectivity. In M. Bullowa (Ed.), *Before speech: The beginning of human communication* (pp. 321–347). Cambridge University Press.

Trevarthen, C. (2003). Infant psychology is an evolving culture. *Human Development, 46*(4), 233–246.

Vandell, D. L., Wilson, K. S., & Buchanan, N. R. (1980). Peer interaction in the first year of life: An examination of its structure, content, and sensitivity to toys. *Child Development, 51*, 481–488. https://doi.org/10.2307/1129282

Van Laere, K., Peeters, J., & Vandenbroeck, M. (2012). The education and care divide: The role of the early childhood workforce in 15 European countries. *European Journal of Education, 47*(4), 527–541.

Van Oers, B., & Hännikäinen, M. (2001). Some thoughts about togetherness: An introduction. *International Journal of Early Years Education, 9*, 101–108. https://doi.org/10.1080/09669760120053466

Wenger, E., McDermott, R., & Snyder, W. (2002). *Cultivating communities of practice*. Harvard Business School Press.

Whaley, K. L., & Rubenstein, T. S. (2004). How toddlers "do" friendship: A descriptive analysis of naturally occurring friendships in a group child care setting. *Journal of Social and Personal Relationships, 11*, 383–400.

Williams, S. T., Mastergeorge, A. M., & Ontai, L. L. (2010). Caregiver involvement in infant peer interactions: Scaffolding in a social context. *Early Childhood Research Quarterly, 25*(2), 251–266. https://doi.org/10.1016/j.ecresq.2009.11.004

Wittmer, D. S. (2008). *Focusing on peers: The importance of relationships in the early years*. Zero to Three.

Wittmer, D. (2012). The wonder and complexity of infant and toddler peer relationships. *Young Children, 67*(4), 16–25.

Index

Administrative and policy decisions, 101, 102–104
Affection, 30, 32, 34–36, 66
Ailwood, J., 62
Akhtar, N., 49
Andrews, M., 18, 28
Apple, P., 75
Ashby, N., 37
Aslanian, T. K., 62
Attachment relationships, 6
Axtmann, A., 96

Banerjee, R., 98
Barrera, I., 94, 98, 110
Beck, L. M., 83, 86, 87
Bergen, D., 22, 46, 54
Besio, S., 20
Bhavnagri, N. P., 70, 73
Block play, 13, 16, 17, 20–21, 56
Bradley, R. H., 101
Brenner, J., 37
Brock, A., 13
Brown, E., 37
Brownell, C. A., 34, 37, 39
Bruce, T., 15
Bukowski, W. M., 34
Burnett, G., 22
Bussey, C., 101

Caplan, M., 37
Caregiver roles and infant–toddler play, 22–28, 52–57
Chen, D. W., 37
Clowning, 48
Cochran-Smith, M., 87, 89
Cole, P. A., 95, 110
Colley, H., 68

Community-building, 100–101, 109–110
Conflict and relationship-building, 37–39, 41
Constructive play, 20–21
Corsaro, W., 39
Corso, R. M., 94, 98, 110
Cousins, S. B., 63
Cranton, P., 87
Croft, C., 96
Culturally responsive care, 69–73, 80–82
Curricula, 55–56, 97, 106, 108

Dalli, C., 62, 64, 77, 88, 92, 101, 109
Darling-Hammond, L., 86
Davidov, M., 35
Davis, B., 40, 41, 68, 101
Dearnley, D., 68, 86
Degotardi, S., 5, 6, 18, 24, 30, 34, 36, 40, 41, 48, 50, 51, 62, 75, 79, 81, 101, 104, 108
de Haan, D., 16, 101
Demetriou, M., 23, 24, 25
Derman-Sparks, L., 82
Detweiler, A., 96
Dewey, J., 86
DiCarlo, C., 22
Discussion questions
  administrative/structural support, 104
  humor and social exchanges, 57–58
  infant–toddler friendships, 42
  infant–toddler play, 29
  infant–toddler professionals' roles, 73
  professional development, 90
Documentation, 27–28

Driel, J., 89
Dunham, P., 34
Dunn, J., 31, 34, 68
Dvorakova, K., 6, 36, 40, 100

Early Intervention (EI) services, 97
Eckerman, C. O., 31, 34, 37
Edwards, C. P., 31, 36, 75, 76, 80, 82
Elfer, P., 68, 69, 75, 77, 86
Elicker, J., 75
Emotional labor, 66–69
Empowerment Theory, 45–46, 48
Engdahl, I., 21, 35, 51
Enhancing Brain Development in Infants and Young Children (Bergen et al.), 22
Erdosi, V., 80
Experimentation and exploration, 14–15
Exploration of objects, 16–18
Eyer, D. W., 94

Families
   family development, 101–102
   family-professional partnerships, 95–96
   as primary educators, 93–95
Feiman-Nemser, S., 87
Field-based experiences, 83–84
Fincham, E. N., 6, 7, 22, 72, 80, 102, 103, 107, 109
Fogel, A., 5
Formosinho, J., 28
Foss, M., 65

Gallo-Fox, J., 89
Gattis, M., 53
Gazing and social play, 33
Gerhardt, S., 66
Gloeckler, L., 6, 75, 108
Goldschmied, E., 15
Goldstein, L. S., 63, 64, 65, 67, 68
González, M., 96
Gonzalez-Mena, J., 23, 70, 72, 73, 94
Goodfellow, J., 40
Goodnough, K., 89
Goouch, K., 6, 88, 104, 106

Gopnik, A., 65
Gordon Biddle, K. A., 16
Greve, A., 21
Grossman, S., 68, 69
Gupta, A., 73

Hamilton, C. E., 6, 77, 101
Hammond, R. A., 26, 106
Hännikäinen, M., 21, 51
Hartup, W. W., 30, 32, 37
Hay, D., 31, 37
Hill, D., 101
Hochschild, Arlie, 68
Hoicka, E., 49, 53, 56
Honig, A. S., 76, 77
Horm, D. M., 74, 83, 107
Howes, C., 6, 32, 34, 36, 40, 77, 101, 104
Hoza, B., 34
Hughes, A. M., 16, 17
Hughes, B., 28
Hyson, M., 107

Imitation, 14, 21–22
Inclusive education, 96–98
Infant–toddler friendship, 3–4, 30–42
   sociocultural context, 36–39
   supportive caregiving, 39–42
Infant–toddler humor, 4
   classroom support for, 52–57
   definitions and overview, 43–45
   peer encounters as catalyst, 50–51
   theories of, 45–46
   types of, 46–49
Infant–toddler play
   caregiver roles, 22–28
   observation questions, 28
   play experiences, 15–22
   and ways of learning, 13–15
Infant–toddlers
   as active social agents, ix, 1–2
   rights to responsive and loving care, 107–109
Infant–toddler teachers
   mentoring and peer co-reflection, 88–90
   primary caregiving, 74–77

Index

professional development, 84–85
reflective practice, 86–88
roles, 61–73
skills required, 77–82
supportive learning communities,
82–90
teamwork, 85–86
Institute of Medicine and National
Research Council, 5
IOM/NRC (Institute of Medicine
and National Research Council),
106
Isik-Ercan, Z., 88

Jackson, S., 15
Jacobson, T., 69
Jarvis, Pam, 13
Joint attention, 33–34
Jung, J., 6, 23, 27, 83, 88, 89, 106

Kemple, K. M., 39
Kitayama, S., 70
Kopp, C. B., 39
Kuhl, P. K., 106, 108

Lake, V. E., 67, 68
Lally, J. R., 5, 6, 62, 75, 77, 104, 106,
107
La Paro, K. M., 6, 75, 108
Lee, L., 22
Lee, S. Y., 5, 36, 76, 77, 79, 104
Lee, Y. J., 82, 83, 96
Lerner, C., 95, 110
Lewis, M., 32, 34
Licht, B., 37
Lillemyr, O. F., 15
Lindahl, M., 21
Locke, John, ix
Loizou, Eleni, 2, 4–5, 20, 21, 23, 24,
25, 26, 27, 45, 46, 48, 52, 53, 83,
84, 86, 106
Løkken, G., 17, 34, 48
Love
and ambivalence concerning touch,
66–67
as component in caregiving, x,
61–66

Lucas, T., 31
Luckner, J., 98
Lytle, S. L., 87, 89

Manning-Morton, J., 64, 77, 83
Margetts, K., 75, 76, 77
Markus, H. R., 70
Martin, S. N., 56, 89
Materials/toys, 55–56. *See also* Block
play; Exploration of objects
McCormick, K., 104
McDevitt, S. E., 72, 82, 98, 99, 103
McGaha, C. G., 32, 41
McGhee, P., 45, 49, 57
McMullen, M. B., 75, 104, 109
Meltzoff, A. N., 18, 106, 108
Mentoring, 88–90
Mezirow, J., 87
Miller, K., 32, 34, 36
Miller, P., 100
Mireault, G. C., 44
Montessori, Maria, ix
Moore, C., 34
Morrissey, A-M., 19
Movahedazarhouligh, S., 17, 19
Mozere, L., 109
Mueller, E., 31, 37
Muir, E., 78
Mundy, P., 33
Murphey, D., 98
Murphy, C., 89
Murray, C. G., 66
Mussatti, T., 30

National Scientific Council on the
Developing Child, 105, 107
Neilsen-Hewett, C., 37
Nemeth, K. N., 80
Newell, L., 33
NICHD (National Institute of Child
Health and Human Development),
75
NICHD Early Child Care Research
Network, 5, 104
Nicholson, S., 83
Nilsson, P., 89
Nimmo, J., 83

Noddings, Nel, 64, 92
Norris, D. J., 83

Observation, 14
  powers of, 77–79
Open-ended toys, 17. *See also*
  Exploration of objects
Osgood, J., 67
Owen, S., 6, 103, 106, 109

Page, Jools, 27, 62, 63, 64, 65, 66, 68,
  76, 77, 86
Park, S., 83
Parten, Mildred, 16
Partyka, T., 23, 25, 27
Pearson, E., 5, 6, 18, 30, 36, 48, 50, 51,
  75, 79, 81, 104, 108
Peer co-reflection, 88–90
Peer-play interactions, 21–22
Perino, O., 20
Peterman, K., 31, 37
Peterson, S. H., 106, 108
Petrie, S., 6, 103, 106, 109
Phillips, D. A., 5, 75, 78, 104, 106
Piaget, Jean, 16
Piaget's developmental theory, 31
Piper, H., 66
Powell, S., 6, 88, 104, 106
Pramling Samuelsson, I., 21
Pretend play, 18, 19–20, 56
Primary care system, 74–77
Professional development programs
  (PDPs), 84–85
Puig, V. I., 88, 89
Purper, C. J., 68

Quiet-time observation, 26–27, 85

Raikes, H., 31, 36, 75, 76, 79, 80, 104
Rausch, A., 27
Ray, A., 83
Recchia, Susan L., 2–3, 5, 6, 7, 15, 22,
  23, 26, 27, 36, 39, 40, 64, 65, 66,
  72, 74, 75, 76, 77, 79, 80, 82, 83,
  84, 85, 86, 87, 88, 89, 92, 94, 96,
  98, 99, 100, 102, 103, 104, 106,
  107, 109

Reciprocal social play, 30, 32–33, 35
Redder, B., 40, 41
Reddy, V., 44, 47, 48, 52, 54–55, 57
Reflection, 27–28, 69
  peer co-reflection, 88–90
  reflective practice, 86–88
Reifel, S., 83
Relationship-based frameworks
  to build community, 91–104
  and family development, 101–102
  guiding principles, 6–7
  human relationships, prioritization
    of, 92–93
  overview, 2, 5–6
  and primary care system, 74–77
  visions for future, 105–110
Relationships
  attachment relationships, 6
  authentic and meaningful, 5–6
  relationship-building process, 79–80
Repetition and imitation, 14
Riley, D., 35
Rita Gold Early Childhood Center,
  3, 4
  guiding principles, 7
Ritchie, S., 6, 40, 101, 104
Rochat, P., 36
Rockel, J., 63, 83
Role-play, 19–20
Ross, H., 37
Roth, W., 89
Rousseau, Jean-Jacques, ix
Routines, 23–24
Rubenstein, T. S., 109
Rutanen, N., 21

Salamon, A., 32
Scaffolding approaches, 23, 27
Scantlebury, K., 89
Seland, M., 107, 108, 109
Sheridan, M. D., 16, 21
Shin, Minsun, 1, 2, 3–4, 5, 6, 21, 23,
  25, 27, 32, 33, 34, 35, 36, 39, 62,
  63, 66, 77, 83, 86, 88, 98
Shonkoff, J. P., 5, 75, 78, 101, 104, 106
Singer, E., 16, 45, 46, 50, 101, 107
Sleep routines, 71, 94

Index

Slomkowski, C., 34
Smilansky, Sara, 16
Smith, H., 66
Snaider, C., 66
Social play, 18–19
    reciprocal, 32–34
Structured play, 25
Swim, T. J., 88

Te One, S., 107
Theory of the Absurd, 45–46
Thompson, R. A., 101, 106
Tobin, K., 89
Tomasello, M., 33, 34
Tomlinson, H. B., 107
Tortora, S., 26
Touch, physical, 66–67

Toys/materials. *See* Materials/toys
Transitions, navigating, 98–100
Trevarthen, C., 18, 78

Vandell, D. L., 31, 32, 34, 101
Van Laere, K., 62
Van Oers, B., 21, 51

Watch, Wait, and Wonder (WWW)
    philosophy, 78–79, 85
Wenger, E., 89
Whaley, K. L., 109
White, J. E., 40, 41
Widemeyer-Eyer, D., 23
Williams, S. T., 41, 94, 98, 106
Wittmer, D. S., 14, 18, 19, 30, 39, 40,
    106, 108

About the Authors

Susan L. Recchia, PhD, is Professor Emeritus at Teachers College, Columbia University, where she served as coordinator of Early Childhood and Early Childhood Special Education programs and faculty director of the Rita Gold Early Childhood Center. Her interests in research and practice include preparing professionals to work with infants and young children and their families, inclusive early childhood education, and building caring childcare communities.

Minsun Shin, EdD, is an associate professor in the Department of Teaching and Learning at Montclair State University, New Jersey. She is the graduate program coordinator for MAT Early Childhood Education Programs. With a strong belief that education takes place in and through human relationships, her research interests include social development among young children, infant caregiving, caring pedagogy, early childhood teacher education, and professionalism in early childhood care and education.

Eleni Loizou, EdD, is a professor of early childhood education at the University of Cyprus. Her research interests include infancy, play, and humor. In her teaching and research, she aims to take young children's perspectives and to consider the impact of teachers' interaction with children and involvement in play. She uses the outcomes of her research to inform early childhood teachers' training and to guide her teaching courses.

Printed and bound by CPI Group (UK) Ltd, Croydon, CR0 4YY
31/07/2025